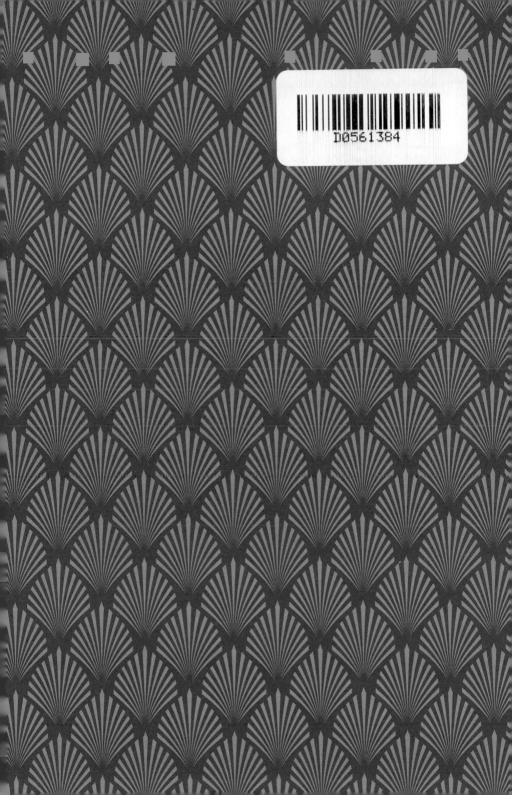

THE
MANHATTAN

Also by Philip Greene:

To Have and Have Another:
A Hemingway Cocktail Companion

THE
MANHATTAN

The Story of the First Modern Cocktail
WITH RECIPES

PHILIP GREENE

Foreword by Dale DeGroff

Photographs by Max Kelly
at Death & Co., Post Office Whiskey Bar, and OTB

STERLING EPICURE
New York

STERLING EPICURE
New York

An Imprint of Sterling Publishing Co., Inc.
1166 Avenue of the Americas
New York, NY 10036

ISBN 978-1-4549-1831-8

Distributed in Canada by Sterling Publishing Co., Inc.
c/o Canadian Manda Group, 664 Annette Street
Toronto, Ontario M6S 2C8, Canada
Distributed in the United Kingdom by GMC Distribution Services
Castle Place, 166 High Street, Lewes, East Sussex BN7 1XU, England
Distributed in Australia by NewSouth Books
University of New South Wales, Sydney, NSW 2052, Australia

For information about custom editions, special sales, and premium
and corporate purchases, please contact Sterling Special Sales
at 800-805-5489 or specialsales@sterlingpublishing.com.

Manufactured in Malaysia

4 6 8 10 9 7 5

sterlingpublishing.com

Cover design by Elizabeth Mihaltse Lindy
Cover photographs by Max Kelly
Interior design by Christine Heun

For Elise

CONTENTS

PART TWO: THE DRINKS

FOREWORD

n 2005—a year and a few months short of the 200th anniversary of the birth of the cocktail—the Museum of the American Cocktail opened in the French Quarter of New Orleans. We carefully assembled a group of passionate and somewhat eccentric cocktail authorities, including collectors, historians, a Hollywood graphic designer, spirits experts, writers, and a young trademark attorney from Washington, D.C., named Philip Greene. The goal was to celebrate a truly rich aspect of our culture: the American cocktail. Assembled from our unusual collections of bottles, gadgets and tools, memorabilia from the film industry, and rare books, the inaugural exhibit told the story of the cocktail from the now famous definition in 1806 through the golden years of the 1880s and then Prohibition and into the twenty-first century.

Why open the museum in New Orleans? It was partly because Phil Greene—who, by the way, happens to be a distant relation of Antoine Peychaud of Peychaud's Bitters fame—argued that New Orleans was the most logical location, the very heart of café society in the nineteenth century, when émigrés from the French Caribbean colonies, Creoles, and Americans gathered in stately saloons and coffee houses. Historians, notably Greene among them, have since established that, despite lore still circulating there, the cocktail wasn't born in New Orleans—but that doesn't matter. The drinking culture of the Crescent City is so integrated into the experience for visitors and so integral to New Orleans culinary culture that there's simply no contest. It's absolutely the perfect place to celebrate the distinctly American culinary tradition of the cocktail.

Many cocktails are native to New Orleans, but the one on which Mr. Greene has set his sights in this book is decidedly not one of them. New York City lays claim to the Manhattan, but is that claim valid? Greene's detective work takes us on a journey that unearths entertaining bits and pieces from newspapers around the country. He builds a colorful tapestry of politics and invention that illustrates the impact that one cocktail had on cocktail culture at large, even showing how that other icon, the Martini, may have spun off from the Manhattan.

In *The Joy of Mixology*, Gary Regan floats the idea that the Manhattan is more than a recipe; it's a category. With the exception of the Old-Fashioned, the Manhattan is arguably the most successful and the longest lived of the strong, stirred cocktails. Greene gives us the formula that illustrates the jump from "old fashioned" cocktails to the new, the modern, when he quotes Theodore Proulx, author of *The Bartender's Manual*:

Manhattan Cocktail

This is made the same way as any other cocktail, except that you will use one-half vermouth and one-half whiskey in place of all whiskey, omitting absinthe.

Greene's point is reinforced in O. H. Byron's *The Modern Bartenders' Guide*. Byron provides two Manhattan recipes and this one-line note instructing bartenders how to prepare the granddaddy of the Martini:

Martinez Cocktail

Same as the Manhattan, only you substitute gin for the whiskey.

Bartenders have returned over and over to this modern cocktail formula for inspiration. Greene mines that rich ore of Manhattan variations and shares those riches in a cornucopia of drinks that vie for a piece of the Manhattan's glory. Some variations embrace the outer boroughs, the Brooklyn and the Bronx for example, others the more recent trend of taking their names from the neighborhoods of New York.

Among my favorites is Vincenzo Errico's Red Hook, the variation that began the neighborhood-versus-borough battle. That drink wonderfully pairs the spicy Carpano Punt e Mes with rye whiskey. In a later recipe for the Bushwick variation, Phil Ward—a veteran of three great cocktail bars: Pegu

Club, Death & Co., and Mayahuel—uses Carpano Formula Antica, not available when the Red Hook graced the Milk & Honey menu. Chad Solomon, a craft bartender who cut his teeth under Audrey Saunders at Pegu Club, introduces Cynar, the Italian artichoke aperitivo, to 100 proof bourbon in his variation, the Bensonhurst. The two get along so well that the Bensonhurst has been welcomed onto cocktail menus far beyond the Brooklyn neighborhood, as have many of the other variations in this book.

What makes *The Manhattan* so entertaining is Greene's light touch, sense of humor, and above all his passion for the subject and all its colorful history. With this compelling, well researched volume, Greene joins a small but distinguished group of drinks historians that includes Gary Regan, David Wondrich, Ted Haigh, Jeff "Beachbum" Berry, and Lowell Edmunds, among others, and I for one look forward to accompanying him on his next journey of discovery.

—Dale DeGroff

OPPOSITE: The Chrysler Building at night

INTRODUCTION
MEET THE MANHATTAN

"There is no such thing as bad whiskey. Some whiskeys just happen to be better than others. But a man shouldn't fool with booze until he's fifty; then he's a damn fool if he doesn't."

—William Faulkner

For the vast majority of the nineteenth century, the "cocktail," that iconic American invention, was a simple affair: Defined in 1806 as "spirits of any kind, sugar, water and bitters," it lumbered along in workmanlike fashion, varied only by the type of spirit or bitters used. A whiskey cocktail, brandy cocktail, gin cocktail—all essentially were the same, and none merited a more particular name. In the 1830s, the landscape got a little cooler with the arrival of ice, but other than that not much innovation was taking place. When Dick & Fitzgerald published the first bartender's book in 1862, Jerry Thomas's *How to Mix Drinks or the Bon-Vivant's Companion*, only ten of the concoctions were true cocktails. The rest were versions of punch, that centuries-old stalwart, along with cobblers, daisies, juleps, sangarees, smashes, sours, and other kinds of libations. All fine drinks, mind you, but they lacked a certain sophistication and liquid eloquence.

Then came the Manhattan, and everything changed. No other drink can match the historical and cultural significance of *the* classic cocktail, the Manhattan. Its advent represents a watershed moment in cocktail history. For the first time, an imported, fortified, aromatized wine known as vermouth modified the structure of the cocktail, adding balance, nuance, sophistication, and sweetness to the base spirit. It completed the revolution and launched a new epoch. The Manhattan so changed the drinking landscape that the original became old hat, old school . . . the Old-Fashioned. This new, blissful union of spirit and vermouth inaugurated a new generation of aromatic drinks, including the Martini which, after all, is a variation on the theme: It uses a different spirit, gin, and dry vermouth. Countless variants of the Manhattan have sprung forth, as you will see, and you can make countless more with a little knowledge and inspiration.

In *The Stork Club Bar Book* (1946), the inimitable Lucius Beebe writes, "make no mistake about it: the Manhattan was the archetypal short mixed drink and blazed a trail for all others to follow." More recently, my friend Gary Regan called it "The drink that changed the face of cocktails.... Quite simply, when properly constructed, it is the finest cocktail on the face of the Earth."

Cheers to that!

Harry Craddock at the American Bar of the Savoy Hotel in London

THE STORY

ORIGINS

"No married man is genuinely happy if he has to drink worse whisky than he used to drink when he was single."

—H. L. Mencken

We begin our tale in May 1806 not in New York City but about 120 miles north in a little town called Hudson. The local paper, the *Balance and Columbian Repository*, had run a cheeky editorial about a recent election in nearby Claverack. It seems the losing candidate had spent too much money on booze and *cock-tails* in particular. A reader inquired what the editor, Harry Croswell, meant by a "cock-tail," and the editor obliged with a now-famous definition:

> *Cock-tail* is a stimulating liquor, composed of spirits of any kind, sugar, water, and bitters—it is vulgarly called a *bittered sling*, and is supposed to be an excellent electioneering potion, in as much as it renders the heart stout and bold, at the same time that it fuddles the head. It is said, also to be of great use to a democratic candidate: because a person, having swallowed a glass of it, is ready to swallow any thing else.

Thus we have the first known definition of the cocktail: spirit, sugar, water, and bitters. Seems pretty simple—and for the majority of the nineteenth century it was. Occasionally a new arrival came along, such as the Brandy Crusta, circa 1850, which heralded the sour style of cocktails, from which we trace the Cosmopolitan, Daiquirí, Jack Rose, Margarita, Sidecar, Whiskey Sour, and many others. But until around 1875 a true *cocktail* consisted exclusively of those simple four ingredients. The pieces lay there for some time, quietly setting the stage for the dramatic change to come.

Let's take a closer look at that stage.

★

In nineteenth-century America, a handful of cities had bona fide reputations for excellence in food and drink. New Orleans, San Francisco, and New York all vied for prominence as bastions of civilized boozing. New Orleans had its French Quarter coffee houses—the polite term for a saloon—including Hewlett's Exchange, Maspero's Exchange, Old Absinthe House, and Sazerac House; restaurants such as Antoine's, which dates back to 1840; and grand hotels, notably the St. Louis and the St. Charles, later the Grunewald and Monteleone. San Francisco boasted its own great hotels and offered the famous "Cocktail Route, which began at the Reception Saloon on Sutter Street and wound its way to upper Market Street."

But New York's watering holes, its palaces of food and drink, towered over them all, beginning early in the century with the City Hotel, likely the birthplace of the hotel bar; the Albemarle; Ashland House, the reputed birthplace of the highball and notably the Whiskey and Soda; Astor House; the Brunswick; the Buckingham; the Continental Hotel, known for its Whiskey Sours; the Cosmopolitan; Delmonico's; the Fifth Avenue Hotel; Gedney House; Hoffman House, Holland House; the Knickerbocker; Metropole; the Metropolitan; the Oriental Hotel; the Rossmore; Sherry's; the Waldorf-Astoria; and too many others to name. Of these, Hoffman House may have been the most lavish. The celebrated Bar Room was

50 × 70 feet in dimensions, and all of its wood-work, paneling, bar, lunch counters, etc., is of highly polished San Domingo mahogany of the finest quality. The ceiling is frescoed in light colors, and the iron pillars, by which it is supported, are adorned with golden vines that trail in graceful curves around their ebony sides. . . . In the middle of the room is a buffet, 28 feet long and 18 inches wide. This is surrounded by brilliantly polished counters of corresponding length, where may be seen at all hours the citizens and strangers who have dropped in to enjoy a social glass.

Then there were the clubs: Amaranth, Calumet, Century, Knickerbocker, Manhattan, Metropolitan, New York Yacht Club, Pickwick, Union, and others. All were known for their food and drink, particularly the quality of their bartenders. In June 1902, the *New York Times* "With the Clubmen" column observed: "Cooling drinks are among the necessities of every club at this time of the year. Nearly all the clubs in New York have some one drink which has been specially concocted by a member and the recipe of which is sometimes jealously guarded until at last it does become public property."

Ruling the roost at these prestigious establishments were the legendary barmen of the nineteenth century: Cato Alexander, "Curly Headed Billy" Bergen, John Brophy, Thomas Campbell, Harry Christian, J. W. "Handsome" Conroy, James Delehey, D. A. Driscoll, William Henry "Billy" Dugay, Harry Johnson, William Mulhall, William "the Only William" Schmidt, George Seeley, Shed Sterling, Jerry Thomas, Orasmus Willard, and many others. Some of their number became famous, much like today's celebrity chefs. An 1893 story in the *Philadelphia Inquirer* noted that the Only William's book "*The Flowing Bowl,*" has made him famous," and describes him as "several years in advance of the times. William invents a new drink every day." In 1904, the *New York Times* lavishes praise on him for having produced "a Mixture with Astonishing Qualities . . . his masterpiece—the grand cocktail!"

But let's turn the clock back and see how it began with an unlikely marriage of ingredients.

PRE-PROHIBITION VERMOUTH

"But can you tell me where he gets his whiskey?"

"We cannot, Mr. President. But why do you desire to know?"

"Because, if I can only find out, I will send a barrel of this wonderful whiskey to every general in the Army."

—Abraham Lincoln, responding to reports that General
Ulysses Grant drank too much whiskey, as reported
by the *New York Herald*, September 18, 1863

America isn't a melting pot; it's a mixing glass. The country has absorbed and assimilated wave after wave of immigrants—English, Irish, Scottish, German, Italian, Chinese, Scandinavian, and so on—and in the mid-nineteenth century the cocktail world began taking slow note of a new kind of Italian immigrant: vermouth.

Fortified wines (spiced and scented) existed in the ancient world (China, India, Persia, Greece, Rome), but today's sweet vermouth begins in late eighteenth-century Turin. According to legend, in 1786 the young distiller Antonio Benedetto Carpano created "his particular blend of 30 botanicals macerated into sweet, floral Moscato wine." A basket of said wine was sent to King Vittorio Amedeo III of Sardinia. The king embraced it, ensuring its ensuing popularity. In the village of Pecetto, near Turin, a competitor named Cinzano introduced its own offering, and public favor continued. In southern France, Joseph Noilly developed his own paler, drier version in the early 1800s. (The company later became Noilly Prat® when Claudius Prat joined the firm.) Not far away, Joseph Chavasse created Dolin® Vermouth de Chambéry in 1821, "using local alpine botanicals found in the Rhône-Alpes region of southeastern France." Before

I.B. CARPANO

long, Martini y Sola—predecessor of Martini & Rossi®—hit the scene. In Europe, vermouth was on the rise.

When did it reach America? In *Famous New Orleans Drinks & How to Mix 'Em*—a classic but problematic text—Stanley Clisby Arthur presents a red herring of a drink. "According to hoary but unsubstantiated tradition, this was the favorite tipple of General Andrew Jackson, known as Old Hickory, when he was in New Orleans the winter of 1814–15 helping pirate Jean Laffite win the Battle of New Orleans."

Old Hickory Cocktail

1 pony French vermouth [see page 218 for conversions]

1 pony Italian vermouth

1 dash orange bitters

2 dashes Peychaud's Aromatic Cocktail Bitters®

Stir well with ice, and strain into a chilled cocktail glass. Garnish with lemon peel.

A fine tale, but untrue. The drink is worth making, but vermouth hadn't yet reached U.S. shores in 1814. In reality, Italian (sweet) vermouth first arrived at American ports around 1840.

OPPOSITE: Antonio Benedetto Carpano (1764–1815)

Early vermouth ad, *New York Herald*, January 13, 1846

Its French cousin—the drier style, generally imported from Marseille—followed about ten years later. Recipes often call for Italian vermouth or French, which generally means sweet or dry, respectively. But not all vermouths from Italy are sweet, nor are all from France dry. Indeed, the Martini brand (Italy) makes a fine dry vermouth, just as Noilly Prat (France) makes a very good sweet vermouth. But in the broadest sense, French means dry, and Italian sweet.

Shortly thereafter, some early entrepreneurs in Northern California, where another sizeable population of Italian immigrants settled and began making wine, saw an early opportunity to make domestic vermouth, as noted in this ad in the February 1, 1859, issue of the *San Francisco Bulletin*:

But by and large the business of vermouth at this stage was in imports, which increased steadily in the years before and after the Civil War. Jerry Thomas doesn't mention vermouth at all in his watershed book, *How to Mix Drinks or the Bon-Vivant's Companion* (1862), but the fortified wine does make an appearance in a somewhat gushing dispatch from Europe five years later. The May 4, 1867, issue of the *Springfield Republican* features a piece called FROM PARIS. LETTERS FROM A YANKEE ABROAD, telling readers back home of the sites to see, what to do, and the food and drink to sample in the City of Light: "In the Italian restaurant, the waiter will offer you . . . bread from Milan" and "in the Austrian brasserie one finds the most rubicund Englishmen and Scotchmen; they love the good beer, and the vermuth gives them a new sensation."

Vermouth was on the rise.

Ad in the *New York Herald*, April 13, 1869

Before long, recipes for the Vermouth Cocktail appeared in the popular bartender guides of the day, beginning in 1869 with *Haney's Steward & Barkeeper's Manual*:

118.-VERMUTH COCKTAIL.

One wine glass of vermuth; one very small piece of ice; one small piece of lemon peel. Serve in a thin stemmed wine glass with curved lip.

Simple, elegant, sophisticated, delightful.

But the popularity of vermouth started accelerating in the 1860s. Between 1867 and 1889, the Martini, Sola & Cia Company—predecessor to today's Martini & Rossi—exported 612,000 liters of it to America. At first, people drank it by itself, as an apéritif, as in the recipe above. But eventually, inevitably, just as Italians ventured beyond Little Italy to blend into American society at large, so too did Italian vermouth, that plucky upstart from Torino. It soon became a major player in the drinking world.

In 1882 the Vermouth Cocktail made another appearance, this time in Harry Johnson's *New and Improved Bartender's Manual* and with a new supporting cast of modifiers:

79. VERMOUTH COCKTAIL.

(Use a large bar glass.)
Three-quarters glass of shaved ice;
4 to 5 dashes of gum;
1 or 2 dashes of orange bitters;
2 dashes of Maraschino;
1 wine glass of vermouth;
stir up well with a spoon, strain it into a cocktail glass, twist a piece of lemon peel on top, and serve.

Two years later came two further variations in O. H. Byron's *The Modern Bartenders' Guide*:

VERMOUTH COCKTAIL, NO. 1.
(A small glass.)
$1\frac{1}{2}$ pony French vermouth.
3 dashes Angostura bitters.
2   "   gum syrup.

VERMOUTH COCKTAIL, NO. 2.
(Large bar glass.)
$\frac{3}{4}$ glass filled with fine ice.
4 to 5 dashes gum syrup.
1 or 2   "   Angostura bitters.
2 dashes Maraschino.
1 wine-glass vermouth.
Stir well. Strain into a cocktail glass. A piece of lemon peel on top. Serve.

Jerry Thomas offered his two variations in his 1887 *Bar-Tender's Guide*:

VERMOUTH COCKTAIL.
(Use small bar-glass.)
Take 2 dashes of Boker's bitters.
1 wine-glass of Vermouth.
1 quarter slice of lemon.
Shake the bitters and Vermouth with a small lump of ice, strain in a cocktail glass in which the lemon has been placed. If the customer perfers it very sweet, add two dashes of gum syrup.

Vermouth had arrived.

But just as new immigrants cluster together, vermouth didn't assimilate into other cocktails. It took its time. The Vermouth Cocktail, in its several variations above, more or less represented the liquid version of Little Italy. It stood on its own before blending in. As such, it came to be seen as a lighter—meaning lower-alcohol—more sophisticated, more gentlemanly drink before dinner. The *New York Herald* reflected in 1893 that "As bartenders developed a hardier spirit of invention they essayed other liquors than gin and brandy. The whiskey cocktail became a favorite with the grosser palates, the vermouth cocktail established itself as the true preprandial appetizer with gentlemen of nice perceptions and delicate tastes."

One such gentleman was railroad tycoon and multimillionaire William H. Vanderbilt, known to enjoy vermouth cocktails. It was said of celebrated Wall Street tycoon James R. Keene, who owned six winners of the Belmont Stakes, that he "cheers himself to vermouth cocktails because 'they don't break you up.'"

An 1893 New York State Chamber of Commerce report helps explain vermouth's rise in popularity:

A great deal of good work has been done by the importers of Italian produce in making the wines of Italy fashionable here, and they are to be highly commended for their tireless and well-directed efforts. Through the agency of the Vermouth and Manhattan cocktail,

Vermouth is generally used, and if the extensive counterfeiting of well-known brands could be prevented the importations would within a year be easily doubled.

The report further indicated that from 1888 to 1893, the number of gallons imported (in barrels) had increased from 69,210 to 186,010. Similarly, the number of bottles (in cases) jumped from 427,644 to 656,424 during that same period.

In 1890, the *New York Sun* took note of a similar phenomenon, the meteoric rise in the popularity of French vermouth, for which we had the Martinez and Martini to thank:

Within a few years the demand for the liquor has greatly increased, partly because the cocktail habit has steadily grown and vermouth enters into nearly all cocktails. There was a time when the whiskey cocktail stood almost alone in the esteem of the thirsty American public, and it was made without vermouth. Now vermouth enters not only into the whiskey cocktail but into the gin cocktail, the Martini, and the Manhattan. Furthermore, the habit has grown of serving before a heavy dinner a glass of vermouth and bitters.

An 1896 newspaper piece, syndicated across the country from the *New York Sun*, zeroed in on the reasons behind the trend:

POPULARITY OF VERMOUTH.

Increase in Importations Due to the Taste In Cocktails.

New York Sun: Although Italy is the largest wine producing country in the world, the importation of Italian wines and cordials into the United States is comparatively limited. In the past ten years the increase in importations of wines and cordials from Italian ports has amounted to nearly 200 per cent. This gain, however, is not due to any increasing popularity of Italian wines among American consumers, but rather to two very different causes, the large increase in the number of Italian residents and the general utilization of the most popular Italian cordial, vermouth, for that distinctively American drink, the cocktail.

It goes on to say that "Of late vermouth has come to be a necessary ingredient in nearly every cocktail compounded at an American bar. The vermouth cocktail is, of course, well-known, but no less so, perhaps, is the Martini, which is also a vermouth cocktail."

That same year the Republican National Convention took place in St. Louis, and the Gateway to the West was determined to play the impeccable host. The city's powerbrokers keenly knew of the fondness that Republicans held—in that era, anyway—for bending an elbow. These header lines above an article in the May 24 issue of the *St. Louis Republic* nicely capture the city's pre-convention mindset:

BARKEEPERS MUST PREPARE MIXED DRINKS

CONVENTION VISITORS FROM THE EAST WON'T RUN MUCH TO WHISKY STRAIGHT

SOME POPULAR DECOCTIONS

THE MANHATTAN COCKTAIL, THE GIN RICKEY AND VERMOUTH MIXTURES MUCH SOUGHT.

The author of the article went on to say that

> For the benefit of the St. Louis bar keepers, I will state that the
> demand for mixed drinks during the Convention will run chiefly
> to Manhattan cocktails, gin Rickeys, Vermouth mixtures and plain,
> everyday whisky cocktails. . . .The Boston bartenders say the call
> is mostly for Vermouth cocktails in summer, and members of the
> fraternity in Philadelphia tell me the men . . . demand, as a rule, plain
> whisky cocktails and Manhattans.

It may have taken a while for vermouth to catch on, but it didn't take long for
the spirits industry at large to acknowledge the significance of the phenomenon. The 1898 book *Cocktails: How to Make Them* observes that "The original cocktails were all made from Gin, Whiskey or Brandy, and these are the
spirits used in almost every well-known cocktail made to-day. The addition
of Vermouth was the first move toward the blending of cocktails and was the
initial feature that led to their popularity."

Stateside entrepreneurs took note of the money being made from
these foreign imports, and domestic companies duly tried their hands at the
vermouth biz. On June 15, 1899, the *New York Times* reported on "the steady
increase in the amount of vermouth annually exported . . . to the United States"
from Turin, Italy, noting a threefold increase between 1891 and 1898 and
noting that the State Department strongly thought it "advisable for persons
intending to make vermouth in America to spend some weeks in Marseille
and Turin to obtain some practical experience in its manufacture" since "The
vermuth of Turin is the most famous of the varieties on the market." Of
course, learning how to craft vermouth properly takes more than "some
weeks." As expert Otto Jacoby later said, "A quality vermouth product is
produced only by the cellarman who lives with the product and whose life
and professional pride is tied with it."

Once the Manhattan and the Martinez/Martini gained widespread
popularity, both sweet and dry vermouth became ubiquitous in cocktail
recipes. As David Wondrich notes in *Imbibe!*, "It wasn't until the 1880s,

though, that it [vermouth] took off, first with the help of the Manhattan, then, in the 1890s, with the Martini, and then, as the new century opened, with, well, just about everything."

Cocktail books of the 1880s—Johnson, Thomas, Byron, Winter—featured a handful of drinks containing vermouth. Byron's topped the list at six. William "the Only William" Schmidt's 1892 *The Flowing Bowl* had a noteworthy 29 of them, and some were doozies, such as the Brain Duster, Bunch of Violets, Tip Top Sip, and Weeper's Joy. Louis Muckensturm upped the ante to 34 in his 1906 book, *Louis' Mixed Drinks*, and Albert Stevens Crockett's post-Prohibition *Old Waldorf-Astoria Bar Book* contained a whopping 174 drinks featuring vermouth. As David Wondrich puts it, in his ever-colorful prose, "In the first two decades of the twentieth century, vermouth Cocktails multiplied like *Listeria* in warm egg salad."

Popular culture, as determined by world travelers and the literary set, kept pace with the trend as well. A 1904 story in the *Boston Herald* told of the vermouth cocktail's popularity in Monte Carlo, noting that the cost of the drink ($1) was lower than the cost of a bath ($4). "It is therefore cheaper to take cocktails than to bathe, which may account for a good deal one sees at that world famous resort," the article snarked.

Both John Dos Passos and Ernest Hemingway served on the Italian front during World War I, and the characters in their wartime novels drink it, such as in Dos Passos's *Three Soldiers* (1921). In Hemingway's *A Farewell to Arms* (1929), Lt. Frederic Henry sips from a bottle of vermouth while in a Milan hospital bed, recovering from his wounds.

> They left me alone and I lay in bed and read the papers awhile, the news from the front, and the list of dead officers with their decorations and then reached down and brought up the bottle of Cinzano and held it straight up on my stomach, the cool glass against my stomach, and took little drinks making rings on my stomach from holding the bottle there between drinks, and watched it get dark outside over the roofs of the town.

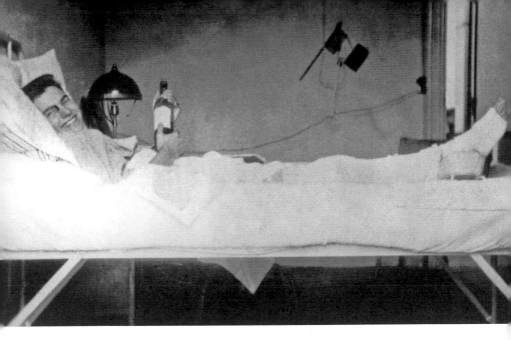

Hemingway, age 19, during World War I

In one of his *Esquire* magazine dispatches from 1935, Hemingway wrote of a drink he invented on the Gulf Stream, composed of a 2:1 blend of dry and sweet vermouth, with Angostura® bitters.

In F. Scott Fitzgerald's *Tender Is the Night,* Dick and Nicole Diver, "as fine-looking a couple as could be found in Paris," enjoyed "a vermouth and bitters in the shadow by Fouquet's bar." In a cheekier example, F. Scott Fitzgerald offered the following post-Thanksgiving recipe to alleviate "the refrigerators of the nation ... overstuffed with large masses of turkey, the sight of which is calculated to give an adult an attack of dizziness:"

Turkey Cocktail

To one large turkey add one gallon of vermouth and a demijohn of angostura bitters. Shake.

But now that we've established the credentials of the Manhattan's key new ingredient, let's look at how the cocktail in question came to be.

MAKING UP
THE MANHATTAN

"You quit drinking that damned Sanka and get on a good Scotch whiskey once in a while! . . . What you need to do is go out and get you about three half glasses of Bourbon whiskey. Then go down to the Occidental and buy a red beefsteak, and then get you a woman."

—President Lyndon B. Johnson to
U.S. Senator Everett Dirksen

Most cocktail experts agree that the drink was invented in Manhattan sometime after the Civil War. But first let's dispense with a couple of theories that put its creation—or at least its perfection—well to the south.

The earliest creation theory takes place in (steady yourself) Bladensburg, Maryland, a suburb of Washington, D.C., on April 17, 1846, at 8:15 a.m. at the old Palo Alto Hotel. According to a story in the December 13, 1908, issue of the *Baltimore Sun,* a resourceful bartender by the name of John Welby Henderson, a native of North Carolina, invented the drink for a shaken-up gent. It seems a dispute had taken place between one John A. Hopkins of Fairfax, Virginia, and Baron Henri de Vrie et Challono, an attaché of the French legation. Gentlemen being gentlemen then, they had but one way to settle the dispute: a duel. But why Bladensburg? According to the *Sun,* "Bladensburg, in those days, was a place of spirited combats and heavy drinking. The old dueling grounds were still in use, and almost daily a party of gentlemen—members of Congress, diplomats or high officials— would come to settle some affair of honor." Call it a case of pistols for two, cocktail for one. On the morning in question, Hopkins and de Vrie, pistols in hand, backs against each other, walked their paces, turned, and fired.

Baron Challono was badly wounded. . . . The ground where he fell
was drenched with blood. His courtly adversary,
Mr. Hopkins, rushed to his side as soon as he fell. Mr. Hopkins, it appears,
was a man of delicate perceptions in spite of his intrepid daring, and the
sight of the Baron's gushing blood made him ill. As a result though he
was not scratched himself, he staggered and seemed about to faint.

Hopkins was taken to the nearby Palo Alto Hotel, where Jack Henderson was
tasked with concocting

something stimulating at once. Jack, a man of reason, saw that
something unusually tempting and powerful was needed. Grabbing
up a Champagne glass, he filled it half full of good old Maryland rye,
and then seizing a bottle of bitters he heaved in a few drops. As he
stirred up the mixture a bottle of sirup caught his eye, and he put in a
swig. Then he pushed the mixture forward—and the first Manhattan
cocktail in the world was born. Mr. Hopkins seized the glass, poured
down the liquor and at once recovered.

The *Washington Post* and New York's *Amsterdam Evening Recorder* also
carried the story, which further noted: "The concoction was originally called
the 'Royal Jack,' in honor of its inventor, but . . . New Yorkers, with their
customary modesty, claimed the drink as their own, and distinguished it from
the old cocktails by prefixing 'Manhattan.'"

La Follette's Weekly Magazine briefly mentioned the story in 1911 in an
unflattering article about Bladensburg:

A half century ago it was a famous watering place and the proprietor
of one of its ancient hotels will today produce long clippings to show
that the immortal Manhattan cocktail was invented in his hostelry
by a distraught southerner there on a mission of honor. Later the
place became a celebrated racing center and then degenerated into a
veritable Sodom, its name banned in polite society.

And as recently as 1954, Old Crow Bourbon Whiskey was using the Henderson story as part of its *Old Crow Almanac* campaign. Offered under the banner "Famous Whiskey Drinks and How They Got That Way," their pitch concludes: "No one seems to know whether Hopkins survived, but the Manhattan did."

A great story, but a hoax. Neither of the two principal characters in the tale existed. In 1908, the *Sun* had an editor by the name of Henry Louis Mencken. In addition to having a fondness for drink, H. L. Mencken, known as "the Bard of Baltimore," had a fondness for hoaxes as well. According to Professor John Baer, a Mencken expert, "If I had to make a guess, it was all made up." A story in Maryland's *Frederick Post* continues:

> Baer, an economics teacher at Anne Arundel Community College [and] . . .
> a Mencken fan for 20 years, said his research turned up no basis for any
> of the purported historical material in the cocktail article. . . . Mencken's
> "vocabulary pattern," writing style and sense of humor show up in the
> cocktail article. Besides, Baer said, the acerbic journalist "was an enthusiast
> for alcoholic beverages." Mencken had apparently been concocting
> libations as well as news stories from his early days as a reporter.

I had the opportunity to speak and correspond with Professor Baer, who confirmed his earlier judgment. "HLM thought that he was a critic of ideas, but he was really a humorist. He wrote about 200 hoaxes which he never acknowledged—most of them in the *Baltimore Sunday Sun* while he was editor . . . between 1906 and 1910. The HLM scholars have yet to discover these hoaxes, but we amateurs discovered them years ago."

Some of those ruses live on. One of his more notorious yarns concerned the bathtub. In 1917 Mencken wrote a story called "The History of the Bathtub," and it was complete hogwash. Among its bogus claims was how President Millard Fillmore's installation of the first bathtub at the White House helped make it more popular to Americans, who initially had rejected it as unsanitary. President Truman cited the story in 1952 while advocating his public health policies, and the object in question was described as a "huge coffin-shaped, zinc-lined, mahogany bathtub" in a puff piece about the Kennedy White House. As recently as 2008, the Kia auto company also fell prey to the deception, mentioning the phony Fillmore bathtub during its "Unheard of Presidents' Day Sale."

But if you were reading Mencken's duel story carefully, you noticed that a key ingredient was missing from the list: vermouth. So let's cross that one off the list and move to the next.

Before we get to the Gotham-based origin stories for our favorite drink, let's address one other theory from beyond the borough, this one from New Orleans. The Crescent City has a reputation for claiming inventorship of all kinds of things, such as the free lunch, craps and poker, the term "Dixie," even the cocktail itself. But this June 20, 1899, story hails from Michigan's *Kalamazoo Gazette*:

MANHATTAN COCKTAIL.

Invented by Col. Joe Walker
Under Pressure of Circumstances.

"The Manhattan cocktail is a delightful appetizer when properly prepared," said a local connoisseur in the art of living, "but it is easily ruined by unskillful hands. It is the invention, by the way, of a native of New Orleans, and the story of its origin is rather curious. Years ago Col. Joe Walker, of New Orleans, was in New York, and went on a little yachting trip with a party of friends. By some oversight the liquid refreshments in the icebox were confined to Italian vermouth and plain whiskey, and it occurred to the colonel that a palatable drink might be made by mixing the two. The result was so good that he experimented a little on his return to New Orleans, and soon perfected the Manhattan cocktail, as it is known today. It was christened in honor of his friends on Manhattan Island, and the fame of the decoction soon spread all over the country."

The *Boston Herald* gave the piece some measure of credibility by mentioning it in passing twelve years later in an item titled "Men and Things" by columnist Philip Hale. Another hoax? Tough to say. Did Colonel Joseph A. Walker exist? You bet your boots he did.

Colonel Walker did in fact walk the Earth. He was a leading citizen of New Orleans, president of the New Orleans City & Lake Railroad, a "large shareholder in the Brewing Association," and—here's where it gets interesting—owner of the famous Crescent Billiard Hall, described in 1875 as "undoubtedly the finest and largest billiard saloon on the continent." At its grand reopening that year, the evening was described as "a scene of enchantment which will pleasantly remain in the memory of the many present to do honor to the occasion. . . . Major Joseph A. Walker, the esteemed proprietor, provided a delicious supper, made up of the rarest dishes prepared in the highest style of art."

November 17, 1852, ad in the *New Orleans Daily Crescent*

BILLIARDS-BILLIARDS.

FALL AND WINTER CAMPAIGN.
GRAND RE-OPENING
-OF THE-
Crescent Billiard Hall.

Having thoroughly refitted with new Cloths, new Balls, new Cues, and new Rubber Matting, the CRESCENT BILLIARD HALL, acknowledged to be the finest Billiard Saloon in the south, and second to none in this country, I beg to announce to the public that I am prepared to meet any and every demand that the taste and comfort of my patrons require.

The CRESCENT BAR ROOM is supplied with the best Liquors and Wines, and daily offers the finest HOT LUNCH served in this city.

The CRESCENT OYSTER COUNTER is now stocked with the choicest Barataria and Cook's Bay Oysters.

J. A. WALKER, Prop'r.

The Crescent Billiard Hall c. 1880 and an announcement from the *New Orleans Daily Picayune*, October 22, 1876

Born in Montreal on December 17, 1842, Walker moved to New York City at the age of four, then to New Orleans at age 24 in 1866. He worked for a time at the St. Charles Hotel, a palace of hospitality, and in 1869 "he engaged in business for himself, opening the famous Bank saloon, and making a mint of money from the start. . . . In 1874 he became the proprietor of Crescent Billiard Hall, which became a leading resort."

So what to make of this story? It's plausible, we can say that. Walker did travel to New York. He was a major player in the hospitality world, and he certainly had a "laboratory," either the Bank or the Crescent, in which to experiment with the "palatable drink" he threw together under pressure in New York. Both whiskey and vermouth were available in New Orleans around this time as well.

But New Orleans newspapers don't mention the Manhattan cocktail at any point before 1890, and the City That Care Forgot does tend to brag about its inventions. Also, why didn't Stanley Clisby Arthur mention this claim in *Famous New Orleans Drinks & How to Mix 'Em* in 1937? The Manhattan's in there, but not a peep about Walker. If anyone was going to tout that story, it's Arthur, an incorrigible homer. He likely created the myth that my distant cousin Antoine Peychaud invented the cocktail in the 1790s. (Peychaud was born in 1803.) But it makes for a good story, so here's to the Colonel and to anyone who believes that the Manhattan was invented in the Crescent City.

THE MANHATTAN CLUB

*"Through the gathering dusk they strolled to the Avenue, where
the crowds, like prisoners released, were walking with elastic
step at last after the long winter, and the tops of the busses
were thronged with congenial kings and the shops full of fine
soft things for the summer, the rare summer, the gay promising
summer that seemed for love what the winter was for money.
Life was singing for his supper on the corner! Life was handing
round cocktails in the street!"*

—F. Scott Fitzgerald, *The Beautiful and Damned*

O
f all the origin stories for the Manhattan, the most popular takes
place at New York's Manhattan Club, circa 1874. One subtheory
involves a reception hosted by Lady Randolph Churchill in honor
of Samuel Tilden, while another concerns club member Judge Charles
Truax. But let's look at the general proposition first: Was the Manhattan
invented at the Manhattan Club?

> Henry Hudson, who discovered 300 years ago the place
> where Broadway's bright lights shine, doubtless also dis-
> covered the Manhattan cocktail.

From the Portland *Oregonian*, March 29, 1909

In the mid-nineteenth century, the Democratic Party opposed a strong
central government and favored a more agricultural economy that suited
Southern planters and the Peculiar Institution—a polite euphemism for
slavery. As such, Southern Democracts supported secession and military
resistance to what they saw as Northern aggression to their way of life. The

party's public image took a hefty beating during the Civil War—even in the North, where it split into factions in favor of war and of peace—and suffered further disrepute after the assassination of President Lincoln in April 1865 and his subsequent near-deification.

The Democratic Party lay in ruins, but New York City Dems still had the wherewithal to establish a social club that year. The Manhattan Club officially formed at a meeting held at the legendary Delmonico's restaurant, located on South William Street in what is now Manhattan's Financial District. Circa 1866, the club relocated to the Benkard Mansion at 96 Fifth Avenue on the southwest corner with 15th Street.

The Manhattan Club had found its first permanent home, and a beautiful one at that, where in time it became known for lavish entertainments. The house became

known as "No. 96" by the members, who picturesquely appear in the annals of early club days as "silk stocking Democracy" attending receptions "in the par excellence swallowtail coat, white choker and light kid gloves. . . ." The Benkard house days, when New Yorkers all knew each other and there was much time for social intercourse, are said to have been the most social years of the Manhattan.

The Benkard Mansion was purchased at a cost of $110,000, a princely sum in those days. The house was

a very handsome residence with a fifty foot frontage on Fifth avenue and a spacious garden on the Fifteenth street side. It was a pleasant old place, whose large front parlor with windows commanding both avenue and street the club took for its reading room. In later years a balcony was thrown out to the rear and converted into a summer dining room, where the members could dine al fresco.

OPPOSITE: The Benkard Mansion on Fifth and 15th

According to an 1893 story in the *New York Herald*

It was in the very heart of the fashionable club district of New York. Directly opposite was the New York Club, the dude club of the day. . . . The Union was only a few blocks above on Fifth avenue. The Travellers, long since passed out of existence, was in the old Cunard house, a block above. . . . By this time, too, the club had acquired a large reputation for an excellent cuisine, wines and cigars.

But let's not forget the drinks. Both its bar and its bartender, John F. Irish, also had an excellent reputation. The *New York Herald* offered that "Politicians and statesmen who lounged in the smoking room of the Manhattan Club have reason to thank John F. Irish when they wake up with a dark brown taste in their mouths." A backhanded compliment perhaps, but it's important to note a culture of inventing drinks at the Manhattan Club, as happened at many of Gotham's clubs. In 1873, this item ran in the *New York Sun*:

The great American drink appears to be a cocktail and more of them are sold to cultivated drinkers than all other drinks together. They are made of every imaginable liquor, from gin to champagne, and so hit every stomach. A good many drinks are invented in club houses. The New York club has a peculiar cocktail. It is made of the best brandy and several kinds of bitters, and they always want it shaken in ice, not stirred. The Amaranth club has a cocktail made with seltzer, and the Manhattan club has invented another.

Of course, we don't know exactly what this drink contained. Seltzer perhaps? We have to wait another nine years for the earliest known reference to the Manhattan cocktail, which appears in the *Olean Democrat,* an upstate New York paper, on September 5, 1882:

Talking about compounders of drinks reminds me of the fact that never before has the taste for "mixed drinks" been so great as at present and new ideas, and new combinations are constantly being brought forward. It is but a short time ago that a mixture of whiskey, vermouth and bitters came into vogue. It went under various names: Manhattan cocktail, Turf Club cocktail, and Jockey Club cocktail. Bartenders at first were sorely puzzled what was wanted when it was demanded. But now they are fully cognizant of its various aliases and no difficulty is encountered.

The earliest direct connection between the club and our cocktail comes in 1889 from a "Boston bartender who stated that 'the Manhattan cocktail originated in the mind of the drink mixer at the Manhattan Club's rooms in New York.'" Then another connection: An 1893 item in the *New York Herald*, concerning the club's membership, noted that "There are the young gentlemen who sometimes break glasses, but always drink oyster and Manhattan cocktails."

NEW BEVERAGES.

It is now the style among the swells of the Manhattan Club to open dinner with an oyster cocktail and close it with a frapped cafe royal. These are new drinks to the "deah boys."

The frapped cafe royal is a peculiar drink. It consists of three-fourths of black coffee and one-fourth brandy, frapped in a cooler, and drunk while the mixture is yet in a semi-frozen state. It is very potent.

From the *Tacoma Daily News* of March 11, 1891

On April 2, 1893, the *New York Herald* discussed the club's downstairs oyster bar: "This, too, is the lair of that famous institution of the Manhattan club, the oyster cocktail. The genius who invented this delight, like Excelsior, must go nameless down to fame, as must the Indian sauce which the artist adds as the last of the eighteen ingredients to the mixture. It is something hot and cooling, mild but stirring, bitter yet sweet." The story goes on to discuss the club's "open bar" policy, noting that "The Union and other big clubs long since gave up the open bar as dangerous, the idea being that the time it took a waiter to go back-and-forth from the sitting room to wherever they need drinks and private might suffice to lead the member from the error of his ways." But quite the contrary at Old 96: "we have the bar room of the Manhattan as free as air, and while I'm about it I may as well say that an old fashion applejack cocktail—a most insidious and stem winding beverage—is generally accounted the correct thing to top off an oyster cocktail with."

Two points in this piece stand out. The author doesn't call the Manhattan Cocktail "that famous institution of the Manhattan club," but rather the oyster cocktail. Further, when he does mentioned a drink by name, it's the "old fashion applejack cocktail." Odd.

A month later, however, the *New York Sun* came to the rescue with a lengthy article on the club, its history, membership, political activities, and of course the drinks:

> The best whisky is sold there at 10 cents a glass. It is the best in the market, and even at ten cents a glass there is a profit to the club. Cigars are sold at 10 percent over cost. The best whisky is sold at other places at 25 cents a glass, and the profit on cigars in some of the swell hotels and cafes uptown is sometimes nearly 30 percent. You can get the finest dinner in the land at the Manhattan at prices which are 25 percent below those charged by Delmonico. More famous drinks have been invented at the Manhattan than at any other place in the country. None ever manufactured was so popular as the Sam Ward, and is made of yellow Chartreuse, cracked ice and lemon peel. The famous Manhattan cocktail was invented at the club. This consists of equal portions of vermouth and whisky, with a dash of orange bitters.

A couple of other political stories tie the cocktail to the club, suggesting a more than passing association between the two. A political column written in 1886 notes that the club's members haven't embraced or even heard of socialism. "There is a rumor that they believe the new era requires the substitution of dynamite for Angostura bitters in mixed drinks, and hence their fright." A tenuous connection, to be sure, but it all goes on the scales.

In the other story, Carter Harrison, former mayor of Chicago, landed in hot water when he allegedly made disparaging comments about president-elect Grover Cleveland. According to the story, after a Saturday night reception at the Manhattan Club on November 19, 1892, Harrison stayed into the wee hours, drinking Manhattans and "talking spitefully" of Cleveland. When the latter man heard the story, the future twenty-fourth president reportedly said: "It is an outrage. An outrage."

"ONE MANHATTAN COCKTAIL."

THE TRIBUNE appears to have been misinformed as to the doings of Mr. Carter H. Harrison at the Manhattan Club early last Sunday morning after the Cleveland dinner. So far from making uncomplimentary remarks about Mr. Cleveland and Ben T. Cable and Adlai E. Stevenson at 2 o'clock in the morning, as was reported, he "left the club before 12 o'clock, was in bed at 12:30," and could not have made uncomplimentary remarks concerning the gentlemen named, as he is a "great admirer of Mr. Cleveland," has "most kindly relations with Mr. Cable," and is "a warm, personal friend of Mr. Stevenson."

From the *New York Herald*, November 22, 1892

In his own defense, Harrison asserted that he met briefly with some gentlemen and "took one Manhattan cocktail with them. It does not take very long to drink a Manhattan cocktail, and the few minutes I sat there were chiefly taken up by a Republican who was giving the reasons that had induced him to vote for you [Cleveland]. I left the club before 12 o'clock and got to my hotel five minutes after 12. By half-past 12 I was in bed and asleep."

Whiskey had long been associated with the Manhattan Club, but beginning in the late 1880s, when the drink was becoming entrenched in bartending manuals, a Manhattan Club brand of bourbon emerges. There were countless other brands of whiskey on the market, true, but the pieces form more than just the sum of their parts.

W. J. VAN SCHUYVER & CO.,

Wine and Spirit Merchants,

No. 63 Front St. - - - - - Portland, Oregon

Cyrus Noble Bourbon!   Old Hickory Bourbon!

Manhattan Club Bourbon!

Ads such as this were common in
Portland newspapers in 1888 and 1889.

The connections continued into the twentieth century as well. For example, the *New York Times* of June 29, 1902, says flat out: "Legend states that it was the Manhattan Club which first gave birth to the Manhattan cocktail." On August 28, 1915, the *Milwaukee Sentinel* reported that "The Manhattan club of New York is preparing to celebrate, in October, the fiftieth anniversary of its founding. . . . If our memory for historic dates is accurate, the club celebrated its twenty-fifth anniversary by giving to the world the Manhattan Cocktail." (Unfortunately, if you do the math, you'll see that their memory isn't accurate—at least as far as the *Olean Democrat* and the Winter and Byron bartender's manuals are concerned.)

We've established a solid connection between the club and the cocktail, but now we come to a fork in the road. In one direction: Tilden; in the other: Truax.

Let's turn first to the Tilden tale, which appears to have originated in a 1945 column by Patrick Murphy as part of his "The Barman's Corner" series that ran in the *Catering Industry Employee* trade journal:

From out of Manhattan last week came data from Ed Gibbs, one of the trade's way-back-when columnists and now a publisher and newsletter writer, to the effect that the Manhattan Cocktail has a definite date of origin. If so, this will be one of the very few cocktails which can be nailed down as to time and place of birth. The Gibbs' version, which in turn is from sources he labels as his "research department," declares that on a memorable December 29, 1874, evening at the Manhattan Club, "in the old A. T. Stewart Mansion— now the Empire State Blg.," a testimonial dinner was held in honor of Samuel J. Tilden. This is the Tilden, history-wise readers will recall, who received a majority vote of the U. S. A. when Presidential candidate, but was defeated by the electoral college set-up. Official notes on the banquet alluded to declare that the dinner was preceded by a drink made of "American Whiskey, Italian Vermouth and Angostura Bitters. It proved so popular that club members asked for it again and again, hence became known as the Manhattan Cocktail."

This reads well but we must remain a bit dubious. For instance, it is quite probable that the drink was served before that December 29th evening in the Manhattan clubrooms—it may have been the house drink of several years. And old bar guides, one that we have being originally printed in 1860, list many a Manhattan Cocktail, so the name antedates the event Mr. Gibbs speaks of.

Murphy is right to remain dubious, as he says. First, the reception held on December 29, 1874, didn't take place at the old Stewart mansion because the club didn't occupy that house until around 1890. Second, no "old bar guides" existed in 1860. Jerry Thomas came first in 1862 but delineated the Manhattan only in the 1887 edition of his book. Besides, the recipe made its debut in 1884 in George Winter's *How to Mix Drinks*, Joseph W. Gibson's *Scientific Bar-Keeping*, and O. H. Byron's *The Modern Bartenders' Guide*. Samisch & Goldmann, the publisher of Harry Johnson's *New and Improved Bartender's Manual*, made the bizarre claim that his book had first appeared in 1860, seemingly trumping arch-rival Jerry Thomas.

Perhaps Murphy mistakenly thought that the Thomas and Johnson books both appeared in 1860. But either way, it isn't so.

The Tilden story gained yet more traction in 1950 when this item appeared in Walter Winchell's column syndicated to more than 2,000 papers worldwide:

* * *

HOW IT BEGAN – On Dec. 29, 1874, in the lordly mansion which had been the home of Lady Randolph Churchill, mother of Winston Churchill, by then and still the Manhattan Club, a dinner was held to honor Samuel Tilden, who had cleaned up the nefarious Tweed Ring of Tammany, and was about to be inaugurated governor of New York. For the occasion a bartender, whose name has escaped eternal fame, concocted a new appetizer – of rye whiskey, sweet vermouth and bitters. It spread around the world as the Manhattan cocktail.

* * *

Jack Lait, who occasionally made guest appearances in Winchell's place, wrote this piece, as it appeared in the *New Orleans Times-Picayune* on August 20, 1950.

In the decades since, popular legend has added an additional twist to the Tilden tale, namely that Lady Randolph Churchill—née Jennie Jerome, a New York socialite and heiress—not only hosted the reception but instructed a bartender to create the drink in honor of the occasion. Seems pretty compelling: a drink created in Manhattan, at the Manhattan Club, by the mother of an avowed whiskey drinker, and named the Manhattan Cocktail. Of course. But does the story hold water?

Let's take a closer look.

In addition to its reputation for drinks and oysters, the Manhattan Club was known for its grand receptions. They were legendary. The May 8, 1874, issue of the *New York Daily Graphic* describes the Manhattan Club as "the head-centre of the aristocratic Democracy of the nation. This is where the great Democratic lights meet to drink champagne, eat woodcock, and lay down the rules and regulations to govern the whole Democratic party."

So did the Manhattan Club ever host a reception for governor-elect Tilden?

Indeed it did, more than one, including a huge reception on December 29, 1874, as this story in the *Albany Argus* confirms:

> DEMOCRATIC REUNION. The Manhattan Club Reception. Honors to Gov. Tilden and Mayor Wickham. Congratulatory Speeches and Letters. The reception given Governor Tilden and Mayor Wickham by the Manhattan Club on Tuesday evening was a grand affair. A large number of distinguished Democrats were present from all parts of the Union. . . . The capacious rooms of the Club House were packed to their utmost capacity, and the best feeling prevailed among the vast throng."

So far, so good. Now what about Lady Randolph Churchill?

As David Wondrich notes in his excellent book *Imbibe!*: "This story, one of the most widely propagated of all drink myths, could hold up, except for the fact that the inaugural celebrations happened to coincide with Lady Winston's delivery and christening of baby Winston—in Oxfordshire." In other words, Lady Randolph Churchill couldn't have attended the reception.

Maybe she invented the drink—and said nothing about it to anyone ever—before sailing for Britain. Another theory worth considering holds that the reception in question didn't take place on December 29, 1874. As mentioned earlier, the Manhattan Club often held political receptions for Tilden. Here's a quick overview of those that took place in the mid-1870s.

APRIL 8, 1874: "the Manhattan Club gave two notable receptions, the first, April 8, 1874, to Democrats from all over the country; the second, in December of that same year, to Tilden and Wickham on the occasion of their election to the offices respectively of Governor

of New York State and Mayor of New York City." —*New York Sun*, October 10, 1915

MAY 6. 1874: "There is to be a conclave of politicians at the Manhattan Club . . . tomorrow evening. It is thought that the meeting will be in the interest of Samuel J. Tilden for governor." —*Cleveland Plain Dealer*, May 5, 1874

"The old Democracy lately had one of their spasmodical reunions at the Manhattan Club, in New York, and celebrated the recent victories of their party." —*New Orleans Daily Picayune*, May 15, 1874

NOVEMBER 5. 1874: "A spontaneous, hearty, large and representative gathering of Democratic leaders from as many states as could be reached, convened in the rooms of the Manhattan Club in New York last night. . . . There were speeches made by Mr. Samuel J. Tilden, Governor elect." —*Brooklyn Daily Eagle*, November 6, 1874

"Three hundred gentlemen of the bluest democratic blood gathered from all parts of the United States in the old Benkard mansion, corner of Fifteenth street and Fifth avenue, to celebrate, congratulate, and cherish each other on the victory won by the democratic party in nineteen states over the foe who had beaten them since 1861. . . When Mr. Tilden entered in evening dress, and having a widely stretching white necktie, as straight as the vertebra of a sword fish, the gallant old gentleman was congratulated as Governor." —*Indiana State Sentinel*, November 10, 1874

DECEMBER 29. 1874: "The first reception at the Manhattan Club to Governor Tilden and Mayor Wickham, a few weeks ago, was as lively as a bottle of champagne just uncorked at the club's table. But the second reception, which occurred last evening, was as dull and flat as a bottle of champagne uncorked overnight and found on the table amid the wreck of the supper next morning after the guests had gone home and to bed. . . . The *World's* eighteen columns' report this morning of almost unrelieved twaddle may be searched in vain for any satisfactory assurance of what the democrats are going to do, or that they are doing or intending anything—beyond giving receptions to the Governor-elect and the Mayor-elect at the Manhattan Club." —*New York Evening Post*, December 30, 1874

MARCH/JUNE 1875: "The Fitz Porters of the Manhattan Club announce that they will give a reception to the democratic Senators of the present Congress. This is to be another champagne and truffles glorification." — *New York Herald*, March 15, 1875

"The Manhattan Club of New York City gave Samuel Tilden a little reception on Saturday night last." —*Indianapolis Journal*, June 14, 1876

OCTOBER 30, 1876: "The Manhattan Club will give Governor Tilden a reception this evening." —*Daily Graphic*, October 30, 1876

Throughout all of these stories of receptions at the club, we find no reference to Lady Randolph Churchill or that she had anything to do with the creation of the cocktail. Nor do these or any other newspaper accounts of the receptions mention any signature cocktail being served. But absence of evidence isn't evidence of absence—and so we turn to Truax.

According to a different story, the cocktail came to exist at the request of a prominent member of the club, Judge Charles H. Truax. So said the judge's daughter, Carol Truax. But in a 1963 issue of *Gourmet* magazine she indicated that the drink was invented by "some anonymous genius" at the club.

The record shows that one Judge Charles H. Truax did exist (thankfully for Carol), and he served as president of the club in 1900. According to a 1915 story on the club's fiftieth anniversary, "Judge Truax was a great traveler and a dominant factor in local politics and often called upon to solve factional problems and a noted gourmet. The wines of his celebrated private cellar were too rare for duplication." He also was "famous as an after dinner speaker."

In his 1988 book, *Villas at Table: A Passion for Food and Drink*, James Villas adds flesh to Carol's story:

> For years enthusiasts have believed that the Manhattan was created
> in 1874 by a bartender at New York's Manhattan club especially for a
> banquet given by Lady Randolph Churchill (mother of Sir Winston)

Charles H. Truax

to celebrate the election of Governor Samuel J. Tilden. Well, after having been put in touch with Carol Truax, a prolific octogenarian food writer who states in one of her twenty-seven cookbooks that none other than her father, Supreme Court Judge Charles Henry Truax, came up with the drink when he was president of that club around 1890, I'm now ready to dispute the long-time theory. "It's true that the old Manhattan club on lower Fifth Avenue was originally the home of Jenny Jerome (Lady Churchill)," said Miss Truax, "but she really had nothing to do with the invention of the cocktail. What really happened was that my father, who was very fat, would stop his carriage at the club every day on his way home from court and drink a few Martinis (two at a time, since they were two for a quarter!). When the doctor told him he absolutely had to cut out the Martinis if you hoped to lose weight, he swiftly dropped by the club, told the bartender they had to come up with a new cocktail, and the Manhattan was born—named after the club. Of course, when he later returned to his physician, heavier than ever, and told about the delicious substitution for Martinis had come up with, the doctor roared, 'But that's even worse!'"

You'll have spotted the yarn spinning on the wheel by now. In 1963, she told *Gourmet* that "some anonymous genius" invented the drink, but 25 years later it's dear old dad who had it made. Let's ask first: Was Truax even a member of the Manhattan Club at the time? As we've seen, the first print description of the drink occurs in September 1882, but the October 10, 1880, issue of the *Irish American Weekly* ran a story about a Tammany Hall meeting to discuss a proposed slate of candidates, including Truax for judge of the Superior Court. The paper identifies him as "about 37 years of age," a graduate of Hamilton College, and "a member of the 'Knickerbocker Club.'"

The first reference that connects him to the Manhattan Club dates to June 7, 1883. It seems more than a little unlikely that he would belong to the Knickerbocker as recently as 1880, switch to the Manhattan Club, develop enough influence there to orchestrate the invention of a drink, and popularize it enough to reach Olean, New York, by September 1882.

So where does that leave us? While it's possible, perhaps even probable, that the Manhattan Cocktail was invented at the Manhattan Club, it seems very likely that neither Lady Randolph Churchill nor Judge Truax invented it—but there is another possibility.

= 5 =

A MAN NAMED BLACK

"When you work hard all day with your head and know you must work again the next day what else can change your ideas and make them run on a different plane like whisky?"

—Ernest Hemingway

Of all the Gotham-based origin stories for the Manhattan cocktail, the Manhattan Club commands the most attention if judged only by volume. A smattering of other stories put its creation at Delmonico's, the Knickerbocker, Jack's, and other watering holes, but the most plausible and serious contender lies in this statement, printed in *Valentine's Manual of Old New York*: "The Manhattan cocktail was invented by a man named Black, who kept a place ten doors below Houston Street on Broadway in the sixties—probably the most famous mixed drink in the world in its time."

Valentine's collected articles, editorials, essays, vignettes, and other writings on the history of New York City. Pieces include "Passenger Barges on the Hudson," "Street Names Which Have Been Changed," "A Memory of Old Harlem," and, of interest to us, "The Golden Age of Booze," penned by a barman named William F. Mulhall. It's in this unassuming article that Mulhall quietly drops the bombshell. But should we take the claim seriously? Who was this Mulhall character?

He was about as legit as they came. In the words of the *New York Evening World*:

> Mr. William F. Mulhall, the head bartender at the Hoffman House, is the most proficient artist in his line in the metropolis. At any rate, his repertoire is something almost phenomenal and his services are regarded as so valuable that they are in demand both day and night.

His cocktails are particularly seductive and it is his success in this direction which has made them among the most popular drinks served at that bar patronized by connoisseurs.

The *New York Herald* glowingly described him in 1886 as "Billy Mulhall of the Hoffman, fabricator in chief of the soothsome 'sour,'" claiming a year later that his "silver fizzes [carbonated cocktails made with egg white] are things of beauty and joys until the next morning." So Mulhall was one of New York's finest bartenders of the day.

But what to make of his claim about a man named Black? As cocktail historian David Wondrich has determined, a George Black owned a place at 493 Broadway until his death in 1881. But describing it as "ten doors below Houston" is a bit of a stretch; 493 Broadway lies nearly three blocks below Houston, near the intersection with Broome Street.

FOR SALE – The popular lunch and sample room formerly owned and conducted by George Black, known as Manhattan Inn, No. 439 Broadway, near the corner Broome st.

The executors of the estate of George Black, deceased, will receive proposals for the above property, with lease running two years from May 1, 1881, which are to be for a sum over and above the cost price of the stock and fixtures, or in gross for the stock, fixtures, lease and good will of the above named property.

Sealed proposals will be received by the executors, at the office of George F. Martens, Esq., Attorney, 261 Broadway, until Tuesday, June 14, 1881, at 12 o'clock noon.

The executors reserve the right to reject any and all bids. Terms of sale strictly cash.

For further information inquire on the premises.

June 11, 1881, ad from the *New York Journal*, lending credence to Mulhall's claim about a George Black having a place on Broadway not far from Houston

View of east side of Broadway, looking north from Broome Street, in 1920

But here the track goes cold. I could find no other trace of an establishment owned by Black in the 1860s or 1870s or one by the name of that Manhattan Inn during that time frame.

Throughout the 1860s, city directories tell of other businesses occupying the multistory building; for example: Thomas Bruns's Engravers for wedding invitations and the like, Frederick Myers's real estate firm, a men's furnishings company run by Joseph Bendix, and hats by Charles Webb.

So, after careful research and much deliberation, should we stick to the various accounts placing the drink's origins at the Manhattan Club, or should we believe the eminent William Mulhall that George Black invented the Manhattan in SoHo? As with so many cocktail tales, the definitive answer remains elusive. It's enough to drive a man to drink.

6

EVOLUTION OF
A CLASSIC

*"My kingdom for a glass of whiskey; I have just dined at the
White House."*

—James Blaine, secretary of State under
President Rutherford Hayes, a teetotaler.

n New York, the Manhattan cocktail "reigned supreme at the Hoffman House.
It came in an infinite number of varieties, and bartenders had to keep track of
special formulas required by regular customers. It was the drink of the substantial man." In 1883, the *Boston Herald* effused: "A Manhattan cocktail, by the way,
is a very good drink just before dinner. It is the ordinary vermouth cocktail with
a foundation of first-rate Bourbon whiskey. I do not advise the *Boston Herald*
readers to drink anything, but, if they will drink, I think they will agree with
me that a Manhattan cocktail is about as good as anything that can be manufactured." Its popularity ranged from New Orleans, where it was deemed "a juicy
and delicious compound," to the Twin Cities, where it made the *St. Paul Daily
Globe*'s 1886 list of "Drinks Which Make a Man Feel Like a King."

Even Confederate general Jubal Early enjoyed tipping them back in
Lynchburg, Virginia. The *Atlanta Constitution* reported in 1895 that

> at the Norvall-Arlington saloon he is a regular caller. Before breakfast
> he enters the saloon, and resting his elbow upon the counter, says: "A
> Manhattan cocktail." His order is useless, for every barkeeper in Lynchburg
> knows the general's drink, and many of them begin concocting the
> Manhattan as soon as he is seen entering the door. A dozen times a day or
> more he imbibes the drink, and swallows it with an evident relish. He has
> been known to teach the barkeeper the secret of making a Manhattan.

So what was the secret?

★

As we've seen, the Manhattan began gaining national recognition by the mid-1880s. In 1883 it appears on the menu of Chicago's renowned Palmer House—for 15 cents! Later that year, the *Chicago Tribune* ran an interview with a bartender named Tommy, who commented on the popular drinks of the day, including the Gin Fizz, Old-Fashioned, and Whiskey Sour. "Manhattan cocktails are in demand, too. I introduced them some time ago and they have become quite popular. . . . I used to keep a bottle of it compounded and serve it out regularly." A *New York Herald* interview with a bartender named William—most likely "the Only William" Schmidt—reveals that "Vermouth cocktails, or 'Manhattans' as they are known all over the world wherever moist pleasure is dispensed, are the most drunk of all mixed drinks."

But pity the poor readers, who had no printed recipes for this delightful new drink. We had to wait until the following year for it to appear in not one but two bartender manuals. First, George Winter's book, *How to Mix Drinks: Barkeepers' Handbook:*

Manhattan Cocktail

(Use large bar glass.)

Two or three dashes of Peruvian bitters;

One to two dashes of gum syrup;

One-half wine glass of whiskey;

One-half wine glass of Vermouth;

Fill glass three-quarters full of fine shaved ice, mix well with a spoon, strain in fancy cocktail glass and serve.

OPPOSITE: The Hoffman House bar, 1890

Then not one but two from O. H. Byron's *The Modern Bartenders'*
Guide:

Manhattan Cocktail, No. 1.

(A small wine-glass.)

1 pony French vermouth.

1 pony whisky.

3 or 4 dashes Angostura bitters.

3 dashes gum syrup.

Manhattan Cocktail, No. 2.

3 dashes Curacoa.

2   '   Angostura bitters.

½ wine-glass whisky.

½   '   Italian vermouth.

Fine ice; stir well and strain into cocktail glass.

Jerry Thomas gave us his recipe in his classic *Bar-Tender's Guide* a few
years later, in 1887:

Manhattan Cocktail.

(Use small bar-glass.)

Take 2 dashes of Curaçoa or Maraschino.

1 pony of rye whiskey.

1 wine-glass of vermouth.

3 dashes of Boker's bitters.

2 small lumps of ice.

Shake up well, and strain into a claret glass. Put a quarter of a slice of lemon in the glass and serve. If the customer prefers it very sweet use also two dashes of gum syrup.

The next year we have *The Bartender's Manual (Revised Edition)* by Theodore Proulx, who took a different approach in describing how to make both a Manhattan and a Martini:

Manhattan Cocktail

This is made the same way as any other cocktail, except that you will use one-half vermouth and one-half whiskey in place of all whiskey, omitting absinthe.

By characterizing the drinks as "made the same way as any other cocktail," he's confirming that the Manhattan was an evolved version of the Whiskey Cocktail (later known simply as the Old-Fashioned) with vermouth costarring. That also explains the presence of gum syrup in early Manhattan recipes. It was a legacy ingredient until makers and drinkers realized that we didn't need the extra sweetness. (As a side note, cocktail bibliographers believe that an 1884 edition of Proulx's book existed, but it doesn't survive, so we can but speculate what that earlier book might have contained.)

Rounding out the decade, we have the recipe from Harry Johnson's 1888 *Bartenders' Guide*:

Manhattan Cocktail

(Use a large bar glass.)

Fill the glass up with ice;

1 or 2 dashes of gum syrup, very carefully;

1 or 2 dashes of bitters (orange bitters);

1 dash of curacao or absinthe, if required;

½ wine-glass of whiskey;

½ wine-glass of vermouth;

Stir up well; strain into fancy cocktail glass; squeeze a piece of lemon peel on top, and serve; leave it for the customer to decide, whether to use absinthe or not. This drink is very popular at the present day. It is the bartender's duty to ask the customer, whether he desires his drink dry or sweet.

Note the variety of adjunct ingredients in those early recipes—Curaçao, absinthe, gum syrup, maraschino—as well as a variety of bitters. George Winter puts the ratio of spirit to vermouth at 1:1, Byron has vermouth at 2:1 over whiskey in recipe No. 1, but 1:1 in No. 2. Thomas has it at 2:1, vermouth over whiskey. (True Manhattan aficionados will want to see the appendix for more pre-Prohibition recipes.)

As the twentieth century stretched its legs, the recipe begins settling down into what we now consider the traditional ratio of two parts whiskey to one of vermouth, as espoused by William Schmidt in 1891, Louis Muckensturm in 1906, Jacques Straub in 1914, Hugo Ensslin in 1916, and Patrick Gavin Duffy in 1934. The typical dry Martini became as dry as the Sahara as the 1900s wore on, but not so with our dear Manhattan. As cocktail historian Gary Regan notes, "The 'drying' of the Martini that occurred in the 1940s almost happened to the Manhattan in the 1990s, and some untrained bartenders out there still think that the drink should be made with just a dash or two of vermouth. But to a large extent, cocktail drinkers know that the vermouth should make up at least one-quarter of the drink."

Then we have the question of which whiskey to use: rye or bourbon? O. H. Byron called for "whisky" in his recipes, and, as we saw above, Jerry Thomas called for rye in 1887.

A Sazerac must be made with rye and a Martini with gin, but most recipes from the early days called simply for "whiskey," which is fine because the success and popularity of the Manhattan depends on the ability to tailor it to specific tastes by means of spirit-to-modifier ratios and styles of vermouth, bitters, and garnish. Rye whiskey was popular from Repeal through the 1950s, while bourbon continued as the brown stuff of choice in Manhattans, Old-Fashioneds, Mint Juleps, and other whiskey drinks until the turn of the new millennium.

In the past ten or so years, however, a rye whiskey renaissance has taken place—albeit in the shadow of the larger bourbon rebirth—with rediscovered classics such as the Sazerac and Manhattan acting as standard-bearers. However you prefer to mix it, these are excellent times to be drinking Manhattans.

Next we come to the question of garnish. Lemon peel or cherry?

Again, the earliest indication comes from Jerry Thomas in 1887, followed by Harry Johnson a year later. Both say lemon. By 1895 we see the first cherry, suggested by George Kappeler in *Modern American Drinks*.

Chicago's Palmer House, mentioned earlier in this chapter, claimed to have originated the use of cherries as a garnish. Like so many other cocktail tales, this one starts with excess inventory. In this case, a packaged foods mogul named Colonel Neumeister apparently had "over a thousand cases of the cherries" that he had to move. So "He put a cherry into a Manhattan cocktail which was being served to himself and his friend, Potter Palmer, the foremost hotel man in Chicago, and proprietor of the world famous Palmer House. And right there was born the cherry in the cocktail idea that is now used in every civilized country in the world." Soon, "following the lead of the Palmer House bar, they [cherries] were used in nearly every bar in Chicago, New York, and other cities soon came into line, and in thirty days the fad had extended to the Pacific Coast."

Regardless of whether cherries as garnish spread like wildfire across the country that way, they did quickly become an integral part of the Manhattan experience. In the summer of 1900, in preparation for the Democratic National Convention, Kansas City saloons stocked up on cherries for the onslaught of "thirsty throats" seeking a quick "dust washer." A typical bar had

half a dozen water coolers filled with mixed drinks. If ten men rush in early in the morning and order Manhattan cocktails they get them as quickly as the deft handed bartender can turn the spigot of the cocktail cooler and fill ten glasses with their mixture. He reaches behind the counter, grabs a handful of cherries and slings a cherry in each glass with one movement of his hand.

In 1904, the *New York Tribune Illustrated* reported what it considered "an amusing incident." A "man of Broadway" was put out when his Manhattan was served sans cherry. "Where is the cherry?" he "demanded" of the bartender. Once the cherry "nestled in the bottom of his glass he declared that he was ready to drink a real Manhattan cocktail." The story went on to explain that "the cherry has dropped out of the Manhattan as made to-day at most of the fashionable drinking places," but a barman would be unwise to do so at "a ladies' café," since "a cherryless cocktail comes back as surely as a bad check."

Indeed, some light-humor columnists would have us believe that the cherry was the star of the show. Take for example the turn-of-the-twentieth-century yarn about the "demure and quiet" woman from out west who had "innocent blue eyes, fluffy brown hair, and much independence." One morning at her New York City hotel, she attracted quite a bit of attention by calling room service to order one Manhattan after another. When the number hit seven, the manager intervened and told her that she'd have to leave. "We cannot have any guests here who drink seven cocktails before breakfast," he explained. At which point, she led him into the room, where all seven drinks sat, untouched, on the mantel. Well, *almost* untouched. "'Why—why—I just wanted to eat the lovely brandied cherries that they put in the bottom of the glass!' wept the gentle young thing."

SEIZED BIG RED CHERRIES

Six Thousand Bottle of Maraschinos Taken By Government.

Adulteration the Charge Brought by Federal Officials-Soda Fountain Men and Bartenders to Feel It.

The next time a soda fountain man fixes himself one he will stop and consider the cost before ornamenting it with a Maraschino cherry. Maraschino cherries suddenly became scarcer and harder to get this morning when United States deputy marshals seized 6,426 bottles of them. Already in many clubs and bars the cherry has been eliminated from the Manhattan cocktail, as has the olive from the Martini, and if the activities of pure food inspectors keep up at to-day's rate the red cherries may disappear entirely.

A September 2, 1911, report in the *Kansas City Star* about bogus cherries "misbranded and adulterated" with benzaldehyde

In 1916, *Our Paper*, a Massachusetts newspaper, used the Manhattan garnish as a punch line in a different way. Among a collection of humorous anecdotes ran this vignette:

> A big Western railroad man was on a tour of Montana. He stopped at a small town named Bowler and went into one of the eight saloons.
>
> "Make me a Manhattan cocktail!" ordered the empire builder.
>
> "I'm sorry, sir," the bartender replied, "but I ain't got an onion in the house."

As a final word on garniture: Do *not* ruin your Manhattan with those grocery store–bought, artificially flavored, day-glo cherry monsters. You can find a number of excellent cocktail cherries these days, such as Amarena Fabbri®, Luxardo®, and other artisanal brands. You owe it to your drink and yourself. Also check the label on those premium cocktail cherries. You might not have to refrigerate them. (If you do, the sugars may crystalize—which won't hurt you or the cherries, but it looks odd.)

7

DRINKER BEWARE

"He spent an hour drinking the drink that Leiter had told him was fashionable in racing circles—Bourbon and branch water. Bond guessed that in fact the water was from the tap behind the bar."

—Ian Fleming, *Diamonds Are Forever*

The *Olean Democrat* assured us that bartenders knew their way around a Manhattan cocktail. Barkeeps "at first were sorely puzzled what was wanted when it was demanded," but by 1882 they were "fully cognizant of its various aliases and no difficulty is encountered."

To quote Hemingway, "Isn't it pretty to think so?"

In fact, it took several decades for the bartending community to figure out, en masse, how to make a proper Manhattan. Take for example the poor chap who tried to enjoy one in "a little Connecticut town" in 1889. He wandered into the hamlet's only hotel and headed for its humble bar. When he ordered a Manhattan, he should have spotted the warning signs. Not only did the locals look up "with an air of surprise on their bucolic countenances," but "the bartender seemed dazed for a moment." Those, dear readers, are two very good signs that you should give swift and serious thought to changing your order.

But the bartender soon rallied and began making the drink.

In a large heavy "schooner" glass, he proceeded to place three or four lumps of white sugar, and saturated them with a liberal supply of bitters, enough for a dozen cocktails. Over this he poured some whiskey, added a gill or so of rum, put in a dash of brandy, and poured over all a wineglass of gin. Then he squeezed half a lemon into the mixture, shook it well together, and poured the whole foaming liquid into a beer glass. The prematurely tender young man had seen the operation, and had misgivings as to how the "cocktail" would act upon him, but, with the interest of the town centred upon him, he could not back down. He had called for a Manhattan cocktail; there was a Manhattan cocktail on the bar, and he closed his eyes and drank it. Then he went out into the front room, sat down by the stove, and meditated upon the wickedness of the world.

The bartender preened:

"Did you see that feller from York come in here and ask for a Manhattan cocktail?" he asked the other patrons. "Tryin' to guy me. Thought I was green. But I was on to him like a fly. I fixed him. Gave him everything in the place. Gin, whiskey, rum, everything. Mixed it all up, and gave it to him. Set it on the bar, and he drank it. See him? Didn't know the difference. These fly fellers can't beat me. Manhattan cocktail! Huh! ain't no such thing."

But you didn't have to venture into the sticks to find a bad Manhattan. In 1891, the *New Haven Register* tells of a bar on Broadway that "hired half a dozen American women and put them in white aprons and behind the bar." When one gentleman had the temerity to order a Manhattan, the barmaid assumed he wanted a beer. When he specified Manhattan *cocktail*, "she laughed and snickered, and dived under the bar and fished up the 'Barkeeper's Guide.'"

The result? "Then she found the recipe and the man drank it and paid and went away and looked up a doctor. That establishment went the dusty way to failure."

One of the world's best bartenders is one of my friends, Jack McGarry. You'll find him at the award-winning Dead Rabbit Grocery & Grog in Manhattan's Financial District. He'll make anything you want and serve it with his trademark Irish charm. But you might not have been so lucky in Chicago in 1901, when another bartender named McGarry offered nothing but hostility to a "spectacular young man" who dared to order a Manhattan:

"What is ut?" he asked, with acrimony.

"I want a Manhattan cocktail," repeated the late arrival.

"Ye'll drink whisky, or ye'll not leave this house aloive," said McGarry, jamming the bottle and glass on the counter. And the young man took his liquor straight.

As McGarry made the change, he said in explanation:

"It's the ruin of ye'er constitution a-drinkin' these med-up midicines. I'll not have it on me conscience that wan of yez died in me place after takin' a dose."

The *Boston Herald* offered early praise for the cocktail in 1883, calling it "about as good as anything that can be manufactured." But 30 years later a visiting New Yorker endured a rather different experience at a saloon near Faneuil Hall. "My request was for a Manhattan cocktail. If some of our high toned booze dispensers along the Great White Way could have seen the concoction which was set before me it would certainly have floored them." The drink contained "at least two squirts from four different bottles, then some whiskey and cracked ice," and finally a maraschino cherry. "When it was set before me I gulped it down quickly and went away from there at once. . . . I distinctly tasted ginger in the cocktail."

Prohibition didn't go into effect nationally until 1920, but its seeds had long been flourishing in the Sunflower State. The infamous hatchet-wielding saloon-smasher Carry Nation herself hailed from Kansas. As such, drinkers nationwide had axes to grind against Kansas, as demonstrated in this 1902 item from the *Brooklyn Daily Eagle:*

The people of this country have had to put up with a good deal from Kansas, but there are limits to endurance, and Kansas has just put a severe wrench on the public patience. This last defiance of law and order and custom and liberty and taste is in the appearance of a Manhattan cocktail in the various towns of that dry and restless state. . . . For what do you suppose it is that you get in Kansas when you call for a Manhattan cocktail? Milk! cider! ginger! and a sunflower seed! . . . How shall we revenge? By calling knockout drops Kansas cocktails? . . . Or by sending missionaries into Kansas with ice and bottles to show benighted dwellers on the plains what Manhattans really are?

> A new temperance drink is becoming popular in Kansas. It is known as the Manhattan (Kan.) cocktail, and is made of milk, sweet cider, and a dash of Jamaica ginger, with a sunflower seed dropped in it to make it look realistic.

From the February 27, 1902, issue of the *Cleveland Leader*

That same year, a Brooklyn man went to Philadelphia to see a prize fight. Afterward, he ventured into a nearby saloon to enjoy a Manhattan. "The bartender was puzzled and called the other two dispensers who were behind the bar, into consultation. When the Brooklynite got the drink, as they made it after the consultation, he thought he was poisoned."

Farther west and about a decade later, a patron at a club in Salt Lake City encountered a bartender "who professed to being very experienced but whose pretensions were quickly dashed to the ground." The customer had ordered a Manhattan. "The new bartender, whose years of experience were weighing him down, looked at the gentleman for a moment with a puzzled expression, and then said, 'I'm sorry, but I cannot mix you a Manhattan cocktail. I haven't an egg in the house.'"

= 8 =

THE TALE
OF
BUTTERMILK CHARLIE

"The joy of Bourbon drinking is not the pharmacological effect of C_2H_5OH on the cortex but rather the instant of the whiskey being knocked back and the little explosion of Kentucky U.S.A. sunshine in the cavity of the nasopharynx and the hot bosky bite of Tennessee summertime."

—Walker Percy, "Bourbon,"
Esquire, December 1975

t wasn't just the ingredients that Manhattan drinkers had to watch carefully. In one notorious instance, the cocktail itself had political consequences.

We've all witnessed that moment when the fortunes of a promising political candidate take a turn for the worse—Michael Dukakis, Ross Perot, Howard Dean, et al. For each one, it was something unexpected: the tank, the conspiracy, the scream. For Vice President Charles Fairbanks, it was the Manhattan. In the words of the *Richmond Times Dispatch*, "A Manhattan cocktail involved Vice President Fairbanks in unlimited trouble in the very midst of his period of high political hopes."

As 1907 dawned, life for Charlie Fairbanks looked pretty good. Several years earlier, the former U.S. senator from Indiana had been elected vice president under the wildly popular reformer Theodore Roosevelt. It looked more than likely that Fairbanks would receive the 1908 Republican nomination and also Roosevelt's explicit endorsement.

On May 7, 1907, Fairbanks hosted a luncheon for the president at his home in Indianapolis and allegedly served a Manhattan cocktail as

an apéritif to his guests. Seems innocuous enough. But Fairbanks wasn't a drinker himself and actively had courted the teetotaler vote. According to one report, Fairbanks

was making a bid for the farmer vote by always calling for buttermilk on his automobile tours through the country. At the same time he posed as a great temperance man, and was making a hit with a total abstainers when the newspaper sprung the story that Fairbanks had opened his luncheon to President Roosevelt with a round of Manhattan cocktails, dyed cherry and all. Thus public attention was diverted from the original Fairbanks cocktail (a glass of buttermilk surmounted by a round red radish) and the public was told to gaze on a vice president who, though he himself drank nothing stronger than buttermilk, had the nerve to tender his guests, and among them the President of the United States, such a vicious drink as a Manhattan cocktail. Of course it makes no difference whether Fairbanks serves cocktails at his table, or whether he serves buttermilk. The incident is chiefly valuable and showing that the public press no longer treats the Fairbanks boom as anything but a joke.

The press had a field day. The veep, according to one local reporter who had attended the event, "said he tried the cocktail and couldn't drink it, as it 'tasted too much like varnish.'" The moral of the story? "When an Indianapolis newspaper reporter turns down a Manhattan as not fit to drink, this should be taken conclusively that the V.-P. is innocent!"

Nor did the dogged newspaper men drop the matter, wanting to know how the drink was made, how many were served, what other drinks were served, did the president partake, etc.

OPPOSITE: Charles Fairbanks in 1904

SAY PRESIDENT TOOK A COCKTAIL

Some of Those at Fairbanks Luncheon Sure that Wine Flowed Freely.

INDIANAPOLIS July 3–the Roosevelt luncheon given by Vice-President Fairbanks continues to agitate temperance circles. Some of those at the luncheon say the President ate and drank all that was offered him, but as to the vice president no one saw him touch his glass.

Pawtucket Times, July 3, 1907

The *Pawtucket Times* reported that "The waiters did not allow any of the glasses to remain empty, but kept filling them up from the bottles." One attendee, who wisely chose to remain anonymous, "laughed and replied, 'Oh, he took it all,'" referring to the president.

THE DEADLY COCK-TAIL DID THE WORK

Manhattan Gets Fairbanks in Bad.

Defeated as a Delegate to the Conference Because He Served Cocktails When He Entertained Roosevelt.

Jonesboro Daily Times Enterprise, September 28, 1907

The incident might not seem all that important now, but it had lingering ramifications. TR endorsed Secretary of War Taft over Vice President

Fairbanks for the Republican ticket in the upcoming 1908 presidential campaign. Nor did it end there for poor Buttermilk Charlie. The scandal prevented him from being elected even to a delegate's seat at the national Methodist Conference held later that year.

COCKTAIL COSTS FAIRBANKS SEAT IN THE METHODIST CONFERENCE

Lay Delegates With Prohibition Proclivities Refuse to Send Vice President to the Big Baltimore Church Gathering.

The Fairbanks freefall continues, *Cleveland Plain Dealer*, September 28, 1907

Fairbanks returned to practicing law and, perhaps seeking a measure of vengeance, supported Taft against Roosevelt in 1912. Buttermilk Charlie secured the Republican nomination for vice president again in 1916, but the Grand Old Party lost to Woodrow Wilson, and Fairbanks died two years later, leaving little but the name of the Alaskan city as his legacy.

WORLDWIDE POPULARITY

"Always carry a flagon of whiskey in case of snakebite, and
furthermore, always carry a small snake."

—attributed to W. C. Fields

We Americans are an odd lot. When traveling abroad, we gravitate toward the familiar, and we pine for the creature comforts of home. When in Rome, we don't always do as the Romans do. Returning to her native Brooklyn in 1951 after two years in Europe, actress Rita Hayworth famously told the awaiting press that the first thing she intended to do was to eat a hot dog.

Thankfully more open-minded foreigners did just the opposite. During an American tour in 1885, world renowned Austrian actor Adolf von Sonnenthal made a stop in New York, and he

> was introduced by some of his German-American friends to a number
> of our native mixed drinks, the fame of which had reached him in
> Vienna. The actor confessed that they were spirituous works of art,
> and with the Manhattan cocktail . . . he was so palatably delighted
> that he took the recipe with him across the sea, declaring that the
> Viennese would not believe so delicious a drink could be made unless
> they tasted it.

Sonnenthal later cabled to say that members of his theatre company "had pronounced the Manhattan cocktail a veritable Yankee nectar." In its reporting of the story, the *Chicago Tribune* concluded, "Thus it is that the American barroom gradually subjugates and civilizes the semi-barbarians of the Old World."

In another instance from 1893, the "Maharajah of Kapurthala, while on a tour of the music halls and roof gardens of Gotham the other night indulged in the seductive 'Manhattan cocktail' and the insidious 'gin fizz.'"

As more Americans traveled abroad in the late nineteenth and early twentieth centuries, they encountered the so-called American bars popular in London, Paris, and across Europe. As early as 1886, the *Evening Star* reported that "England is a great place for American drinks," noting that the American Bar at the Crystal Palace offered the Manhattan, along with a few dozen other American "concoctions of our versatile toddy slingers." But within a year, a few eyebrows raised at this dangerous American import. The *London Court and Society* cautioned that the Manhattan was "insinuating and fatal" and "must be approached cautiously, and then only by men who have been under fire." It concluded that "In any match between a man and a Manhattan cocktail you must recollect always that it is about ten to one on the cocktail." Later that year, we learn that "The Manhattan cocktail has been introduced into London through the presence of the [Buffalo Bill] Wild West show, and a late copy of an English paper indicates very clearly that the innermost circles of English society are already stirred to the uttermost."

By 1895, the Manhattan had ventured south of the border, down Mexico way. Filing his dispatch from Mexico City, Stephen Crane assured his readership that if you're thirsty, "it is necessary merely to say that if you go out into the street and yell 'Gimme a Manhattan!' about forty American bartenders will appear of a sudden and say 'Yes, sir.'"

Two years later, the U.S. minister to Venezuela introduced "the seductive cocktail" to the people of Caracas:

> The cocktail, that great American institution which has brought comfort to many a jaded stomach on both sides of the Atlantic, is about to be introduced to our fiery neighbors on the continent to the south of us. The young diplomat . . . has undertaken the missionary work, and if his plans succeed Christmas Day in the South American republic will be gladdened by the persuasive influence of the seductive Manhattan cocktail.

Another two years after that, the Manhattan hit Paris. "Guides of shabby gentility flit about offering their services for the Louvre or Cluny by day, and mysteriously whisper of 'Paris by night;' while the waiters are all glib with a long string of American drinks—'Manhattan cocktails, gin fizz, sherry cobbler, grog Americain'—anything you can get in New York." By 1920, other South American cities, notably Buenos Aires, were enjoying the Manhattan as well as the Bronx and Clover Club.

Some of these exotic destinations might make a passable Martini or Manhattan—but most either wouldn't or couldn't . . . at least not at first.

STRANGE DRINKS ABROAD.

Are Sure to Shock the Taste of Experienced Americans.

"You can hardly realize the strange attempts, which are made to imitate the American mixed drinks in the European hotels and drinking places, which are frequented by American tourists," said a New Yorker, who makes it a practice to take a tour through Europe every year.

From the *Kalamazoo Gazette*, April 15, 1900

The traveler in the story above decided to see for himself "how Manhattan cocktails were made in foreign lands." His experiences in Germany and Austria didn't merit mention, and although in London he "found plenty of places with 'American bars,'" they often offered drinks he'd never encountered in the States. On one particular day, "an intense longing for a cocktail" caused him to venture out on his quest with a fellow Yank. "He piloted me to a big hotel, where he assured me that there was a barmaid who could mix a Manhattan with any bartender in New York."

The barmaid's fingers moved so quickly that they looked like a white streak. She tossed into the tumbler a little of nearly everything in the bar, shook the mixture up in a shaker and poured it into two cocktail glasses, each alleged cocktail having a stiff froth about half an inch thick. All I could say about it was that I had tasted worse drinks, not wishing to discourage my friend, who evidently had the mistaken idea that he was drinking a real Manhattan.

The traveler's luck improved in Paris. While the Manhattans "were not the genuine article, they approximated the American drink more closely than anything I had tasted outside of America." Then, at a hotel in the rue Saint-Honoré near the Louvre, he explained to the manager his "intense desire for real Manhattan." He pointed to the bartender and asked the manager, "Can he mix a Manhattan cocktail?" On that cue, "the bartender placed his hands on the counter, thrust his head forward and said with an unmistakable Bowery accent: "Yah betcher boots he can."

He nodded his head several times and look amused at our astonishment. Then he began tossing into the tumbler the ingredients for two genuine Manhattans. While he was pouring them out, the real thing this time, he told us he had been a bartender on the Bowery. Leaving New York for Europe about two years before he had drifted to Paris. He managed to find employment in this hotel at the "American bar," and he made such a success of it that he not only had a good salary, but a share of the profits besides. We had several Manhattans and then the bartender insisted, Bowery fashion, that we should have "one on the house." These cocktails were the first and only of the real article I had tasted outside of America.

Alas, other traveling Yanks fared less well. Take actor Taylor Granville, who visited London in 1913. He happened upon an "American" bar on the Strand, and

went inside and asked the barkeeper to mix him a Manhattan cocktail. While the barkeeper was *concocting* the drink, Granville looked on in amazement. Finally a glass of pink liquid was set before him.

"Would you drink one of those?" inquired the actor of the barkeeper.

"Sure I would," was the answer. "Why not, sir?"

"Well," said Granville, "you mix up another one and drink it and if you're alive after five minutes I'll drink mine."

It got worse—a lot worse—if you ventured further afield, as the *Miami Herald* reported a couple of years later.

> Americans in Europe and Asia who are unwise enough to patronize "American Bars" so-called, have encountered sundry mixtures wholly unfamiliar to the American palate, and wholly unpalatable, called cocktails. There is an "American Bar" in Calcutta—if its proprietors are still unlynched—at which two rupees, the equivalent of 66 cents or thereabouts, is charged for a mixture mislabeled an "American Manhattan cocktail" and served in a brown glass to hide the fact that it is made of white lead, linseed oil and coloring matter.

When the doughboys ventured "over there" to Europe, to fight in the Great War, the bad luck continued. A well-meaning Brit took his new American friend to a West End bar

> and with the greatest good will presented him with what I had always thought was a Manhattan cocktail. He looked grieved.
>
> "Say," he protested, "what've I done that you should wish this on me?"
>
> "Oh, I thought you'd like something to remind you of home."
>
> "Remind me of home? What d'ye call it?"
>
> "It's a Manhattan cocktail."
>
> "Manhattan nothing! Listen here! If any downtown barkeep pulled this stuff on me and called it a Manhattan, say, I guess there'd be immortality

for that barkeep next day. Manhattan? I laugh. Guess you don't know the first thing about it. Gimme some British ale."

But in time European bartenders did come to master the Manhattan and other classic American cocktails. It was inevitable.

On January 17, 1920, America plunged into the depths of the "Noble Experiment," also known as Prohibition. Hundreds of American bartenders flocked to Europe, Cuba, and elsewhere, hoping to continue their craft in friendlier surroundings. Thousands of American drinkers followed, hoping to get a good drink. As a result, standards improved considerably. In 1930, Constable published the immortal *Savoy Cocktail Book* by Harry Craddock, founding president of the United Kingdom Bartenders Guild. *The Café Royal Cocktail Book* by fellow guild president William Tarling appeared in 1937 and raised the bar again.

GREAT AMERICAN COCKTAIL OFFENSIVE FAILS IN LONDON

By Robert J. Prew
Universal Service Staff Correspondent.

LONDON. Aug. 30.—The great American cocktail offensive, directed against London, has failed. The old-time English saloons put up a heavy whiskey-and-soda barrage before which the New York storm troops, although cleverly led, beat a disordered retreat.

The American attack was conducted by unemployed Manhattan bartenders. They effected a secret landing in England, bringing with them an abundance and variety of munitions. They were confident that they would win with "liquid fire," but despite the refinement of their mixed armory, their propaganda system was weak and the forces of the Scottish distilleries won an easy victory, without having to call out the English beer and Irish stout reserves.

In issuing an official admission of defeat, Harry Craddock, late of Holland house and Hoffman house, New York, and now of the Savoy hotel, London, says: "My New York friends can not break into this town. The Englishman prefers a long drink. He likes to sip his whiskey and soda, not to toss it off quickly. For that reason he can not take to cocktails. Later he may change; it's all a matter of education."

Craddock has 200 cocktails on the Savoy wine list, but 50 per cent of his customers are Americans.

September 1, 1920, story in the *Anaconda Standard* of Montana, decrying the failure of American cocktails to take hold in London during the opening months of Prohibition

Nevertheless, old habits can prove hard to break. In 1933, the year that Prohibition ended, one reporter in Vienna ordered a Manhattan and encountered a monstrosity that in color was "a deep, chocolate brown, and nearly as thick as molasses. In taste it was like the most evil cough syrup that was ever mixed. . . . On the top of the noxious mixture floated a thin slice of raw onion, and beside it swam a small square of white bread."

= 10 =

A PLACE IN
THE PANTHEON

"He had foolishly drunk the two Manhattans the stewardess
had plunked down on his tray. For some reason he drank
Manhattans when he was in the air. Never on the ground.
What significance there?"

—Irwin Shaw, *Rich Man, Poor Man*

f we were to create a pillared pantheon of cocktails, I believe it would consist of the Old-Fashioned, Manhattan, Martini, and the Daiquirí. In 1935, *Brooklyn Eagle* correspondent Guy Hickock averred that the Old-Fashioned was "the most popular of the long list of cocktails, Manhattan and Martini a close second." He also included the Bacardi Cocktail—essentially a daiquirí with grenadine—and the Whiskey Sour in his top five. David Embury, in his essential 1948 book, *The Fine Art of Mixing Drinks*, names the Old-Fashioned, Manhattan, Martini, and Daiquirí as "among our six basic cocktails," the other two being the Jack Rose and Sidecar.

But look at all four of those pillars, and you'll find that, in varying degrees, all but the Manhattan have fallen victim to corruption.

The Old-Fashioned more or less has remained true to its core ingredients—whiskey, sugar, and bitters—but many an unholy concoction has slid across the mahogany under that sacred name. The primary culprit is fruit. Once upon a time, someone decided to add an entire orange and half a cherry tree, muddled beyond recognition, to make a proper Old-Fashioned. Neon-red maraschino syrup? Why not! Have at it, my boy! Others thought it wise to add sugar or even the sin of seltzer water. It's only recently that the drink is getting the recognition and proper handling that it's due.

The Martini now generically describes anything served in a martini glass. To many blasphemers, it doesn't need to contain gin, vermouth, *or* bitters, which entirely defeats the point. At a place where I'd typically drink beer, I met friends for happy hour. The chalkboard out front read: "Martinis $5." *Sure*, I thought, *I'll have a Martini, then I'll switch to beer.* As I was specifying the gin, the ratio, and how many olives—probably sounding to the server like the angel Clarence at Nick's Bar in *It's a Wonderful Life*—she cut in: "Uh, no, sir, *this* is our martini menu." Before my eyes hovered a collection of nonsense containing various expressions of fruit-flavored syrups and other frivolities.

"The sign says martinis are $5. Bring me a classic dry martini, please."

"Oh, *those* are $10."

Not wanting to cause a fuss—and knowing the vermouth probably was older than she was—I ordered a Sierra Nevada®, a decision that I've never regretted.

These days, a daiquirí means pretty much any frozen drink. You can stroll down Bourbon Street or go to your local chain restaurant and order one. What you'll get for your hard-earned money is a cup of alcoholic slush. The Daiquirí proper is made with rum, freshly squeezed lime juice, and sugar or simple syrup. That's it.

But among the Big Four, the Manhattan has held the high ground most successfully. Sure, you can get a bad Manhattan. I've had more than a few, and you probably have, too. Usually you can lay the blame at the foot of stale vermouth, supermarket cherries, or improper technique. But you're not likely to have to endure artificial ingredients or a totally different base spirit, as happens with the Daiquirí or Martini. In our lifetimes, the Manhattan likely will remain a blend of whiskey, sweet vermouth, and bitters. If a bar stocks only one bottle of bitters, it's likely to be Angostura, so you're more likely to get what you ordered. Because the name never took on additional meaning beyond the drink itself, perhaps the Manhattan survived in a way that the other three could only envy.

Chris Hannah, a bartender at the world renowned French 75 Bar at Arnaud's—a must-visit in the Crescent City—offers his thoughts on the resiliency of the Manhattan:

> The Manhattan made it through and out of the cocktail's dark days,
> but it still had to endure what I call the commissary effect. World War II
> and Vietnam caused a lot of our commodities to be mass produced,

leaving many ingredients scarce—most importantly at our liquor distributors' warehouses. The Manhattan never went out of style like, say, the Brooklyn and the Creole, the same cocktail when you swap the Maraschino and Bénédictine. So when the country for the most part stopped importing Maraschino, Bénédictine, and most importantly Amer Picon, all of those people who enjoyed the better-bodied whiskey cocktail were relegated to the Manhattan because we never stopped bringing over vermouth. The Manhattan survived because of the continued availability of its ingredients. That's why the Sazerac never died: We kept making our own Peychaud's and Herbsaint®.

Robert Hess, host of *The Cocktail Spirit* TV show, author of *The Essential Bartenders Guide,* and a fellow cofounder of the Museum of the American Cocktail, observes:

The Manhattan and the Old-Fashioned appear to have been the only drinks that survived through the cocktail desert of the '70s and '80s, retaining the true heritage of the "cocktail" by still being made with bitters. Most bartenders might not really have understood exactly why they were adding a couple of dashes from the dusty bottle behind their bar, but at least they were doing it. Unlike the Old-Fashioned, the basic recipe for the Manhattan hadn't been lost in translation through the decades and was still being made basically the same way. While its younger cousin the Martini had been robbed of nearly all of its vermouth, the Manhattan usually retained an acceptable amount. This is why the Manhattan is one of my safety drinks, which I can have some level of faith in when ordered at most bars. For those times I find myself someplace where even the Manhattan might not pan out, there's always a gin and tonic.

I couldn't agree more, including the G&T. It's hard not to marvel at the staying power of the Manhattan. Perhaps it's because the drink, like its island namesake, is a metaphor for America: a successful blending of diverse components greater than the sum of their parts.

11

A DRINK GROWS
IN BROOKLYN

*"Am going to ask everyone round for cocktails, perhaps
Manhattans. Will then have given to guests something in
manner of grand society hostess, and if everyone wishes to go
to dinner afterwards: why, they may do so. Not sure what
Manhattan is, come to think of it."*

—Helen Jones, *Bridget Jones's Diary*

N ew York City has five boroughs: Manhattan, Brooklyn, Queens,
the Bronx, and Staten Island. The first four have legitimate cocktails named for them, and of those four the latter three essentially
descended from the first. The first to mix vermouth with a spirit, the
Manhattan spawned the Bronx (gin, sweet and dry vermouth, orange juice)
and the Queens (same but with pineapple juice for the OJ).

The Brooklyn poses something of a curious case, however. The earliest
known recipe goes back to 1908, as found in J. A. "Jack" Grohusko's classic *Jack's
Manual: On the Vintage and Production, Care, and Handling of Wines, Liquors, Etc.*

Brooklyn Cocktail

1 dash Amer Picon bitters [See page 123.]

1 dash Maraschino

50% rye whiskey

50% Italian (sweet) vermouth

Fill glass with ice. Stir and strain. Serve.

OPPOSITE: Borough Hall, Brooklyn, 1908

As you can see, Jack nailed it. He created a delicious cocktail, worthy of taking its name from what would be the fourth most populous city in the nation—assuming Brooklyn were separate from New York City. Then, inexplicably, people forgot about it. Perhaps we can blame its lapse into the void, like so much else, on the Volstead Act. As Prohibition came to an end and thirsty Brooklynites drank openly again, the local papers wondered why oh why didn't Brooklyn have its own drink? But it did. They just didn't know Jack.

Notwithstanding Grohusko's fine creation, two years later the *San Diego Union* reported that a lawyer named Henry Wellington Wack had just invented the Brooklyn Cocktail, the poor borough having "struggled along without a cocktail named in its honor." Wack modestly appraised his own handiwork:

> The "Brooklyn" is the nearest approach to the ambrosial nectar of the gods that the magical compounder of liquid ventricular inspiration has so far produced for the gustatory gratification of mankind. It fits the throat like a velvet flame and plumps into one's stomach with a merry laugh. It sharpens the appetite and the wits, and dulls the edge of malice. It sends worry scampering down the alleys of the past. When the "Brooklyn" becomes our national drink, riches and poverty will dance a can-can on the grave of trouble.

The recipe? "Three parts gin, one part French and one part Italian vermouth, one-half or one-third raspberry syrup. Embalm in a shaker of cracked ice and shake the very life into it. Serve repeatedly, smoking cold." When reached for comment, bartenders at the Hoffman House, Waldorf-Astoria, and elsewhere were less than impressed. One of them retorted: "If I lived in Brooklyn, I'd stick to beer."

Then Prohibition came and went, and before you could say Jack Robinson it was 1934, and the people once again were clamoring for a Brooklyn Cocktail. From a letter to the editor in the *Brooklyn Daily Eagle* of January 28, 1934: "'What about a Brooklyn Cocktail,' is a query in our mail. 'There's a Manhattan Cocktail and a Bronx Cocktail,' writes G.V.S. 'Why not a Brooklyn Cocktail?'" It sounded like a good idea to editors who either didn't do their homework or smelled an easy way to increase circulation figures. They made it a contest:

Almost everybody has his or her pet cocktail recipe. Given a little encouragement, we'll start a competition to line up a Brooklyn Cocktail. We'll have a committee of cocktail experts act as judges—and the winners will be presented with cocktail shakers or something similarly suitable to the occasion. What do you say? Would you like to submit your favorite cocktail recipe—and nominate it for posterity as the "Brooklyn Cocktail?" How's about it . . .

How's about it, indeed? Three days later, the paper again "wondered whether it would be a good idea to start a competition for the best 'Brooklyn Cocktail'—with cocktail shakers as such a prize." One Walter F. Wilkinson offered this proposal:

One jigger of good dry gin. One good dash of peach bitters. And a dash of Vermouth (dry) . . . Bill Krause, who adorns the Walnut Bar at the Hotel Towers, offers this entry, by the way. His "Brooklyn Cocktail" consists of ingredients from a list of Brooklyn streets. It is a semi-dry cocktail and makes a grand aperitif. The recipe is:

1 (small) dash Jamaica Rum (Jamaica Ave.)
3 dashes cranberry juice (Cranberry St.)
½ apple jack (Apple St.)
½ cherry brandy or maraschino (Cherry St.)
1 green olive (Olive Court).

Take fresh pineapple, about 3 slabs, cut into squares, place in shaker and mash with maul. Add cranberry juice, Jamaica, apple, cherry, with chopped ice. Shake and serve in cocktail glass over olive. Bill says that two drinks will send you skipping around singing "Brooklyn Bridge is Falling Down, Falling Downnnnnnn."

Throughout 1934 the *Daily Eagle* maintained the borough's interest in their little competition. On February 4, 1934, we learn that

T. Boland, banquet manager of the Granada Hotel at Ashland Place and Lafayette Avenue . . . submits this recipe for the Brooklyn cocktail:

> One-third dry sherry
> Two-thirds London gin
> Dash Angostura bitters
> Squeeze lemon peel.

Then hold tight to your nearest neighbor.

Four days later, the *Daily Eagle* asserted that "Civic pride has been shaken to its very foundations, we hear, by this business of a Brooklyn Cocktail. There's talk of a boycott against Bronx or Manhattan Cocktails until a Brooklyn Cocktail obtains equal rank—and we may even have rioting in the street unless something is done about it." This same article gives a recipe by a reader named "W.J." consisting of "Two parts Dutch Gin, in view of the fact that Brooklyn was once a Dutch village; one part Jamaica rum, with a bow to Jamaica Ave.; one part pineapple juice, with a bow to Pineapple St., and a couple of dashes of orange bitters, in fond memory of Orange St. and the usual icing and shaking."

Two days after that, a savvy reader informed the paper that the *Savoy Cocktail Book*, published in 1930, already had a Brooklyn Cocktail, and wasn't the intrepid *Daily Eagle* aware? "The recipe is one dash of Amer Picon, one dash of Maraschino, two-thirds of Canadian Club whisky and one-third French Vermouth, then shake well and strain into a cocktail glass."

You might expect a newspaper to take its lumps and concede the scoop, but not so the *Brooklyn Daily Eagle*. They doubled down and replied: "That may be listed as a Brooklyn Cocktail but what we want is a recipe approved by a group of judges—one that will really deserve the distinction of being known as the 'Brooklyn Cocktail' . . . your favorite recipe or mine may be just as good or better and methinks we'll get a committee together and do things about it."

The storyline plodded along all that year, and in December the paper threw logic to the wind by reasoning that it was "only logical—and in keeping with the trend of the times—that we should turn to the restaurant keeper and accord him the honor of creating and presenting a cocktail of cocktails, the Brooklyn Cocktail." They nominated "Brad Dewey, of Gage & Tollner's Restaurant, Fulton St.," who had created "the famous Sunshine Special . . . the ideal choice for promotion to that peak of peaks—the honor of being titled THE Brooklyn Cocktail. And here you have it—equal parts of gin and grapefruit juice, with just a little dash of grenadine. Simple—but oh suh-well!"

But as 1934 became 1935, we still didn't have a consensus in Brooklyn about the Brooklyn. No sooner had the *Daily Eagle* raised Brad Dewey's Sunshine Special to the throne of "THE Brooklyn Cocktail" than dissension in the ranks emerged. Not only that, the paper bemoaned the popularity of the drink's elder sibling:

> The bartenders at the Bossert, particularly at the Grill, have been perturbed these latter days about the alarming fact that all the Brooklyn bankers who drop in for their evening apéritif prefer Manhattan cocktails! Dean Hickey of the Bossert bar, to get around this situation, has evolved a Brooklyn cocktail which he hopes will startle the world. The Brooklyn dish: one-third Italian vermouth, two-thirds gin and a dash of bitters. Shake it up and it shakes you up.

Hickey's Brooklyn appeared to satisfy folks for a few years, but in 1937 it all bubbled up again. Brad Dewey wanted revenge, which he extracted by inventing yet another version of the drink: "Dewey . . . tells us that with the new year here is a new Brooklyn Cocktail, made as follows: Two-thirds real Jamaica rum, one-third lime juice and a dash of grenadine. He says that folks generally have switched to the new version."

In a follow-up piece a month later, the *Daily Eagle* confirmed that "Dewey's Brooklyn Cocktail is THE Brooklyn Cocktail, and let us hope this ends, once and for all, the controversy which has been raging over the drink for so long a time. His concoction consists of two-thirds Jamaica rum (but definitely no other rum), juice of one lime and a dash of grenadine or a teaspoon of powdered sugar." In case you weren't reading closely, the drink just got a whole lot sweeter.

But a week later, the *Daily Eagle* couldn't resist stirring the pot again, as noted in their "Around the Tables with Chester King" column: We "apparently precipitated a miniature civil war last week when we extolled the virtues of Brad Dewey's Brooklyn Cocktail." Gustavus Augustus, bartender at Hotel Bossert's 61 Room, wrote in to say that "The real Brooklyn Cocktail . . . consists of one-third Italian Vermouth, two thirds gin and a dash of bitters. Any deviation from that formula is treason." Paraphrasing Dean Hickey, he added the closing instruction: "Shake well, and be shaken."

But more followed.

"What! A Brooklyn cocktail with rum," Joe at the St. George Bar hissed venomously. "I've been tending bar for 20 years and this, my misinformed friend, is the real Brooklyn Cocktail: Jigger rye, one ounce French vermouth, dash of maraschino and a dash of American Picon."

"Bob," who is the mixologist for the discriminating folk at the Towers Hotel, seemed more disappointed in our judgment than indignant. "A Brooklyn Cocktail," said Bob "is so well known it can be made with only one-half French Vermouth, one-half rye, a dash of American Picon and a twist of orange peel."

But after all of this contest silliness and recipes pitched by readers and bona fide bartenders, here's the kicker: The drink "venomously" espoused by Joe at the St. George Hotel's bar now takes credit as the "official" Brooklyn Cocktail recipe, with the St. George as its birthplace. How do you like that?

But of course that's not the end of the story.

In another case of cocktail amnesia, newspapers were telling us in 1945 of yet another attempt at creating what Brooklyn already had in the bag. The *Trenton Evening Times* reported that at a place called Gilmore's the bartender "invented and placed on the bar menu a Brooklyn Cocktail to compete with the famous concoctions named for Manhattan and the Bronx. . . . A Delmonico glass filled with Scotch, two cubes of ice, bitters, one lump of sugar, one green cherry, and one twist of lime peel . . . (In other words a new fashioned old-fashioned)."

DDT, VODKA FOR BUM FANS

By New York News

NEW YORK, Dec. 8-Bronx borough president James J. Lyons, Saturday proposed the following recipe as Brooklyn's official cocktail:
1 spoonful raspberries
$\frac{1}{2}$ pony DDT
$\frac{1}{4}$ tree branch
1 oz. vodka
1 dash Durocher bitters,
and, vinegar to taste
Stir well and pour into Gowanus river.

A snarky piece in the December 8, 1945, issue of the *New York News*, in which the Bronx, home of the Yankees, goofs on Brooklyn, home of the Dodgers, AKA "dem Bums," including their manager, Leo Durocher

The combination of rye or Canadian Club®, dry as opposed to Grohusko's sweet vermouth, and Amer Picon has become the official recipe for the Brooklyn, but that's not to say that everyone endorses it. In a 2012 panel discussion, some of the cocktail world's heavyweights—including Dale DeGroff, Philip Duff, St. John Frizell, Robert Hess, Steve Olson, Audrey Saunders, Angus Winchester, and David Wondrich—took aim at some of the industry's sacred cows.

"This is not a good drink," Mr. Frizell said with unhesitating definitiveness. As the owner of a Brooklyn bar, Mr. Frizell has seen his share of Brooklyn cocktails. Most of said concoctions bend over backwards to make up for the fact that you can no longer buy one of the drink's key ingredients, Amer Picon, in America. "Drinking a Brooklyn makes you think, 'Why am I not drinking a Manhattan?'—a drink for which the ingredients are readily available," he said.

In his book *Imbibe!*, Wondrich concurs that Jack Grohusko's 1908 Brooklyn is the superior drink. "While not in the first rank of Cocktails, it's a solid citizen in the second tier. Grohusko's original, with its Italian vermouth, is far better than the version that has come down to us, which uses French vermouth, something that experts at the time felt mixed poorly with whiskey. They were right."

As a final comment on the "official" Brooklyn Cocktail—the one with rye, dry vermouth, and a dash each of maraschino and Amer Picon—you could say that the drink was invented at . . . yes, the Manhattan Club! A lengthy *New York Sun* article that later appeared in the *Cleveland Plain Dealer* on May 21, 1893, tells of a drink called the Manhattan Cocktail à la Gilbert (page 123), essentially the same drink but without maraschino. Also, just as the Manhattan spawned the Brooklyn, so too did the Brooklyn launch a number of delicious offspring, as you'll see, starting on page 205.

12

"SOMETHING FOR THE LITTLE LADY"

"She let the hot, straight whisky ease and burn and flow over her tongue and in back of her tongue, and she swallowed slowly and felt the bite on her palate, and the warmth of the whisky went into her chest and into her stomach."

—John Steinbeck, *The Wayward Bus*

You might think that a whiskey drink wouldn't appeal to women, but think again. Nor is this is a particularly recent trend. In 1892, William "Billy the Bartender" Dugay, "one of the 'star' bartenders of the Hoffman House for about ten years," noted that "The most popular morning beverage with the ladies is the Manhattan cocktail." (For those keeping score, Dugay made his Manhattan with a 1:1 ratio of vermouth and whiskey and with orange bitters.)

In 1901, the *Kalamazoo Gazette* breathlessly reported on the immoral women of New York City and their taste for hooch: "New York clergymen declare that children are decreasingly in Sunday schools because the wealthy society women of the metropolis are so seldom mothers and expend time and strength in gambling and at balls and social routs," it declared, noting that "the prevalence of the drinking habit among respectable women in New York" was particularly alarming.

In dozens of restaurants of the better class may be found women, ladies, if you will, drinking "high-balls," "Manhattan cocktails," and "brandy and soda." In the hotel in which I live I recently saw two young and pretty women, evidently of entire respectability, enter the restaurant. . . . As soon as they were seated one ordered a "high ball" and the other a "Manhattan cocktail." After having disposed of these they each ordered another of the same kind.

GOTHAM SOCIETY
WOMEN SHIRK
MOTHERHOOD

Startling Facts Revealed by
Millionaire Census.

PREACHERS UP IN ARMS

Bring Serious Accusations Against
Butterflies of Fashion.

WOMEN SPEND TIME IN
DRINKING AND GAMBLING

In Their Pursuit of Pleasure They
Have No Time to Become Mothers.
Homes of Rich Are Practically Childless.

The *Kalamazoo Gazette* of April 17, 1901,
tells of those wicked Gotham women.

A year later, the December 19, 1902, issue of *World's Home Magazine* tells of "The Daring Topics Discussed by New York Matrons," especially those belonging to clubs. The Eclectic Club, "composed of some of New York's most fashionable matrons," had run into some trouble with the sauce. "One of the greatest rows in the history of the club was due to the presence of the insidious Manhattan cocktail at club meetings."

That same year, the *Boston Journal* reported on the shocking news that a "women's bar" had opened in Cannes, where many a woman was ordering Manhattans before lunch.

WOMAN'S CLUB DRINK LIST.

Divided Into Short and Long Classes and Contains All the Favorites.

Special Correspondence
THE NEW YORK TIMES.

LONDON, June 8.—The following is a copy of a notice hung up in the smoking room of one of the best known women's clubs in the West End of London:

SHORT DRINKS.	LONG DRINKS.
Absinthe cocktail,	Brandy fizz,
Brandy cocktail,	Brandy sour,
Bronx cocktail,	Club sour,
Gin cocktail,	Cafe cocktail,
Highland cocktail,	Egg nogg,
Lone Tree cocktail,	Gin fizz,
Martini cocktail,	John Collins,
Manhattan cocktail,	Milk punch,
Pousse cafe,	Royal fizz,
Peachona, (non-alcoholic)	Silver fizz,
Sloe gin cocktail,	Tom Collins,
Vermouth cocktail,	Whiskey fizz,
Whiskey cocktail.	Whiskey sour,
	Stone wall,
	Slings. (various.)

Any Drink NOT ON LIST, please ask for.

From the *New York Times* of June 23, 1912, this is the drink list of one of London's best-known women's clubs.

Then there's this gem, also 1902, from a *Brooklyn Daily Eagle* item called "She Knew Her Drink—Story of a Shy Maiden at Brighton Beach."

She was a sweet young thing with a shy, timid air, which suited her quiet costume and her bloomer hat. When the young man she got acquainted with at Brighton asked her to have some refreshments at a nearby pavilion she hesitated, but at last consented to take something to drink at the restaurant. When they were seated at the table he suggested that as the day was chilly she take something to warm her, remarking that ginger ale might have that effect. After waiting for him to order his own drink so as to give a hint, at last, she said, looking around the restaurant, "what are they drinking at that table? That drink in those small goblets, with what looks like a cherry in it?"

"Oh, that's a Manhattan cocktail," he replied.

"Man-hattan," she said, innocently. "Do women drink that?"

"Why, of course, there are some women drinking them now," he responded, pointing to a couple who seemed to be enjoying the seductive and exhilarating mixture. The shy young thing blushed as well as she could under her tan, and seemed satisfied with the statement. Then turning to her escort, she said:

"Alright, then. I'll take a Hunter straight." And she got it, while the young man looked at her in silent admiration, as she gulped it off.

Hunter, a popular brand, advertised itself as "The highest standard of the American gentleman's whiskey."

Some city women seemed to attract a degree of notoriety from the Manhattan. The March 6, 1901, issue of the *Brooklyn Daily Eagle* reported on the gripping divorce trial of Mr. and Mrs. John Cotton Smith. Trial testimony revealed that the couple had dinner at Gilman's restaurant on Bedford Avenue in Brooklyn, where allegedly Mrs. Smith drank six Manhattans.

"Did you drink six Manhattan cocktails at any time?" Lawyer Kissam asked.

"I never drank six Manhattan cocktails at one sitting. I remember
I had one Manhattan cocktail, but I didn't want to take it. Beckley
Smith suggested it and Cotton Smith said: 'Rose, take it; you need it
after your day's work.' I was not intoxicated."

The 1909 divorce trial of Howard Gould, son of railroad magnate Jay Gould,
and his wife, Katherine, told of even greater excesses. House servants testified that

Mrs. Gould was repeatedly seen under the influence of liquor and that
when she had been drinking she changed from a charming affable
woman to a woman of whims and caprices, ill tempered, not nice in
her choice of language, overbearing and quarrelsome. Mrs. Gould's
one-time personal valet swore that one time he served his mistress
with two quarts of Manhattan cocktails in as many days, besides the
wines and liquors which he said she drank at the table.

After the couple's separation, Mrs. Gould checked into the St. Regis
Hotel. Mr. Gould's lawyers acquired her hotel bills, which reportedly "bristle
with cocktails," resulting in "huge bundles of Manhattan cocktail checks"
being introduced into evidence.

MRS. GOULD'S REFRESHMENT CHECKS.

Here are the checks charged to Mrs. Gould at the St.
Regis from Sept. 24, 1906, to Sept. 28, 1906, both inclusive:

SEPT. 24, 1906.

Time Served.
10:50 A.M.. . . . . . .1 Manhattan cocktail 25
. . . . .1 qt. White Rock. 45
11:31 A.M. . . . . . . .1 Manhattan cocktail 25
. . . .$\frac{1}{2}$ portion ragout of lamb 60
. . . .$\frac{1}{2}$ portion lima beans. 45

```
..............1 piece peach pie...............  .30
..............1 pt. No. 73.................  $2.00
..............1 demi tasse ..................  .20
3:38 P.M.........1 Manhattan cocktail ...........  .25
..............1 pt. White Rock...............  .35
..............1 Manhattan cocktail ...........  .25
7:50 P.M.........1 pt. No. 178 .................  2.25
..............1 Manhattan cocktail ...........  .25
..............1 pt. Apollinaris ...............  .30
..............1 qt. White Rock...............  .45
9:20 P.M.........1 Manhattan cocktail ...........  .25
..............1 Manhattan cocktail ...........  .25
```

SEPT. 25, 1906.

```
11:08 A.M........1 Manhattan cocktail ...........  .25
11:38 A.M........1 Manhattan cocktail ...........  .25
..............1 Manhattan cocktail ...........  .25
..............1 pt. White Rock...............  .30
..............1 Manhattan cocktail ...........  .25
..............1 Manhattan cocktail ...........  .25
7:33 P.M.........1 qt. White Rock...............  .45
..............1 Manhattan cocktail ...........  .25
..............1 pt. No. 73.................  2.00
```

SEPT. 26, 1906.

```
6:20 A.M. .......1 Manhattan cocktail ...........  .25
..............1 English breakfast tea .........  .45
9:06 A.M. .......1 Manhattan cocktail ...........  .25
..............1 English breakfast tea .........  .45
11:55 A.M........1 qt. White Rock...............  .45
..............Manhattan cocktail.............  .25
..............1 pt. No. 73.................  2.00
..............½ portion friend oyster crabs.....  .80
..............1 portion lamb chops............  .85
..............½ portion green corn (cut off) ....  .40
```

From the *New York Times*, June 23, 1909

OPPOSITE: The former Mrs. Gould in 1915

In the early years of World War II, the *Brooklyn Daily Eagle* advised women on how to make popular drinks such as the Manhattan and Martini. "It is true that the man of the house usually takes it upon himself to perform this rite. But this year, with so many men off to the wars, the women will have to make most of the drinks served at Yuletide gatherings." The story patronizingly added: "Cocktail calls have been adding up by leaps and bounds this past week. Anxious feminine voices ask: 'just how do I make such and such a drink?' and add, in a confidential tone, 'you see, I've never made them before.'"

The Manhattan also had a supporting role in the 1959 comedy classic *Some Like It Hot*, starring Tony Curtis, Jack Lemmon, and Marilyn Monroe. Curtis and Lemmon played Joe and Jerry, two 1920s Chicago musicians who had the misfortune of witnessing the St. Valentine's Day Massacre. The musicians decide to dress in drag to avoid detection and join the traveling band of Sugar Kowalczyk, played by Monroe. On a train to their next gig, Lemmon and Monroe share a little whiskey. Lemmon has seduction on his mind, but Monroe plays the mixologist. "We've got bourbon!" she squeals with delight. "We can make Manhattans!" Which they do with a hot water bottle for a shaker and paper cups from the water cooler.

Today, amid the ongoing craft cocktail renaissance, the Manhattan remains popular among elite women bartenders. For example, Lynnette Marrero, cofounder of the SpeedRack competition and owner of DrinksAt6 in New York, notes that a Manhattan

> is a perfect way to enjoy your whiskey. I first tried one at the Flatiron Lounge in 2004. My young palate was not quite ready to drink overproof rye whiskey alone and the vermouth (oh my God, vermouth isn't rancid if properly stored!) and bitters gently mixed by the lovely Katie Stipe was a mind blowing experience. I like brown spirits! The Manhattan keeps getting better and better as more quality vermouths finally get imported into the U.S. I also love playing with the

incredible template; I'll substitute sherry for vermouth, or even split vermouths! Bitters, I am pretty traditional loving the aromatic bitters, but I don't mind when someone adds a couple dashes of Cointreau.

According to Amanda France—executive assistant of the Competitive Enterprise Institute and producer of the *RealClear Radio Hour* and the forthcoming film *I, Whiskey: The Spirit of the Market*—"Whiskey-loving women are on the rise. Whiskey is not just grandpa's spirit anymore. In the United States, women now make up nearly 40% of the whiskey market share . . . The growing number of female whiskey aficionados and drinkers reflects the spirit's surge in popularity." Charlotte Voisey, global portfolio ambassador for William Grant & Sons, adds:

> The Manhattan is . . . a strong, powerful drink that feels laden with history yet ever relevant. It is the first drink you want to have in New York City. As a female there can be something extra empowering about drinking whiskey and Manhattans when for a long time society thought that you shouldn't. That stroke against the norm could make you feel spirit-forward, like the drink.

and, in closing, Francine Cohen, editor in chief of *Inside F&B*, notes that

> Women love whiskey because (when well made) whiskey tastes good. And spirited women have good taste. Why do Manhattans hit a high note with women? If drinks had personality traits this one would scream confidence. It's three simple ingredients, no hiding anything, and what it says is that "I know what I like, and this is it—strong and simple, direct and delicious." Plus, ordering a drink named for a city that everyone idealizes as a place for success infers you're successful for choosing it.

13

POPULAR CULTURE

"Eighteen different kinds of scotch," the stranger said, "including Black Label. And I haven't counted the Bourbons. It's a wonderful sight. Wonderful," he repeated, lowering his voice with respect. "Have you ever seen so many whiskies?"

—Graham Greene, *Our Man in Havana*

One measure of a drink's staying power is the extent to which popular culture embraces it. James Bond's infamous Martini, shaken not stirred, the 1979 Top 40 classic "Escape (the Piña Colada Song)," the Cosmo in *Sex and the City*, and any number of classic cocktails in *Mad Men*, including the Manhattan—you can take the measure of a drink through the lens of how it trends in the public eye, and the Manhattan has a long and illustrious history in that regard: comic strips, movies, even judicial decisions. Fix yourself one, and enjoy these tidbits of Manhattan trivia.

At first, the press took particular pleasure in chronicling the travails of those mauled by the mighty Manhattan. In 1888, the *St. Paul Daily Globe* ran an item titled "Jones Lost His Way" concerning a fellow who wandered into saloon after saloon while seeking directions to the home of a friend. Each time he asked for directions, the friendly barman said, "A Manhattan cocktail is what you want." By evening's end, Jones had consumed no fewer than 19 Manhattans and of course never found his friend's house. "The result shows how many snares lie in the path of innocence in a great city, crooked city," the paper concluded, "for the Manhattan cocktails clung to his brain for several days afterward."

JONES LOST HIS WAY.

Unable to Find Wheeler, He Cultivates Mr. Manhattan Cocktail.

It Was a Long Journey to Zig-Zag Street With Drinks Between.

Every Time He Drank Things Looked Different, You Know.

A Night When the Air Was Full of Angostura Bitters.

From the *St. Paul Daily Globe*, December 2, 1888

Five years later, the waiters of the International Hotel Employees' Association held a picnic, including a cocktail race that symbolically turned Jones's wandering into something rather more sporting. "Every contestant will hold a silver tray on which will be placed a Manhattan cocktail, the glass filled to the brim. At the word go, the men will run or walk as they please around the track. The man who gets around the quickest and spills the least liquor will get first prize. Those who do not win prizes will be allowed to drink their cocktails."

Doesn't sound as though the race had any losers!

The press's early moralizing soon turned to lampooning, however. The *New York Herald* ran a story about a pastor who heard a different kind of calling. The Reverend Julius Feicke left the pulpit to open a saloon in Hoboken. Unfortunately, his mixological skills were somewhat limited. When asked to make a Manhattan, he obliged with a drink consisting of "gum: ½ inch; raspberry syrup: ½ inch; vermouth: three drops; orange bitters: six drops; whiskey: 1 tablespoonful. The result was a mixture which tasted like a grateful cordial often prescribed for infants. It was sweet and bland and oily. And yet that cocktail, combined with a glass of beer, produced a most wearing and riotous effect." When the reporter regained his wits, he noted: "I feel strangely" and wisely crept away.

Similarly, the *Brooklyn Daily Eagle* of January 24, 1902, told of a well-dressed man who apparently had enjoyed far too many Manhattans. When asked, "Where have you been to-night?" the drunken man responded "I don't know. It might have been a wedding, and it might have been a funeral; but whatever it was, it was a great success!"

Humor aside for a moment, the medical community at this time embraced the cocktail. In "The Treatment of Incipient Pulmonary Tuberculosis," which appeared in a 1902 issue of the esteemed *Maryland Medical Journal*, Dr. George C. Johnston advised that "a small Manhattan cocktail a half-hour before dinner will stimulate appetite and digestion." The *Journal of the American Medical Association* offered the same advice the same year. Doctor's orders!

In *State v. Pigg*, one (rather unfortunately named) Robert Pigg was charged with violating a Kansas law against the "unlawful sale of intoxicating liquor." Pigg stood accused of the "sale of two Manhattan cocktails to Leona Larson and Kittie Edie." The trial court found him guilty, but in 1908 he appealed his case on the incredulous basis that there was no evidence that a Manhattan cocktail is "intoxicating." The appeals court's ruling wisely reasoned:

> The Century Dictionary defines a cocktail as "An American drink, strong, stimulating, and cold, made of spirits, bitters, and a little sugar, with various aromatic and stimulating additions." The particular kind of cocktail under discussion is popularly understood to have taken its name from the island whose inhabitants first became addicted to its use. While its characteristics are not so widely known as those of whisky, brandy, or gin, it is our understanding that a Manhattan cocktail is generally and popularly known to be intoxicating.

Consider yourself served.

CAUGHT SIPPING MANHATTAN COCKTAIL.

Danville, Ill. Jan 30. – Detected by members of his con-
gregation while sipping a cocktail in a downtown saloon,
Rev. Charles Devall, an evangelist of Johnson City, Ill, who
had been conducting revival services in the Fourth Church
of Christ here, has suddenly left the city and the meetings
have been closed.

From the *Belleville News Democrat,* January 31, 1908

A humorous item from 1911 tells of the modern conveniences on display in a new, state-of-the-art hotel being planned in Paris "in which all the domestic service will be performed by electricity." Indeed, if a customer "feels like he needs a cocktail, he can touch another button. One touch brings a martini, two whiskey, three a manhattan, four vermouth, five an ambulance. In answer, a dumbwaiter rises through the floor either to bring the desired bracer, or, when need be, to lower the guest to the ambulance."

As the twentieth century raced forward, the drink's popularity reached the echelons of high society. A 1932 story tells us that "The elder J. Pierpont Morgan appeared daily for a Manhattan cocktail after the market closed. And usually limited it to one." But its popularity also extended in the other direction on the social ladder. "When Otto Palm of Cincinnati, got home the other day, he perceived: Four empty glasses, empty vermouth bottle, a depleted supply of cherries, four vanished pints of whisky. Deduced he, in report to police: burglars liked Manhattan cocktails." It turns out that robber barons as well as robbers (well, burglars anyway) liked a proper Manhattan.

Franklin Delano Roosevelt is remembered as a Martini man, but he too was fond of his Manhattans. In fact, while visiting Texas in the spring of 1937, FDR learned that a "spunky 28 year-old Texan had just won a stunning victory" and would soon become a member of the House. Roosevelt "sent for

OPPOSITE: J. P. Morgan in 1915

the new congressman, invited him aboard the presidential special and soon after the two were sharing Manhattan cocktails on a trip to Washington." That junior congressman was future president Lyndon Baines Johnson. In between their respective stints in the White House, we know that Eisenhower liked his scotch and sodas, but his wife, Mamie, was partial to Manhattans— perhaps a little too much. When she'd had a few and got wobbly, her aides invented the story that she had an inner-ear imbalance.

In 1928, Paramount released *Manhattan Cocktail*, a feature film sadly lost to history. Starring Nancy Carroll, Richard Arlen, and Paul Lukas, the film was described at the time as "One of the most diverting and entertaining pictures of the present season. . . . It is a human story of youthful dreams and ambitions. And to top it all, Nancy Carroll sings a number of tuneful, ingratiating songs that are sure to delight her audience." The *Reading Eagle* called it "a moving, thrilling melodrama." We don't know much else about the film, other than it was among the early sound films. (For anyone looking for a connection, Arlen's character was named Tilden.)

But who can forget the classic 1934 film *The Thin Man*, in which William Powell as Nick Charles teaches the bartender the secret of the shake: "You see the important thing is the rhythm. Always have rhythm in your shaking. A Manhattan you shake to foxtrot, a Bronx to two-step time. A dry martini you always shake to waltz time." The Manhattan is the drink of choice in the 1958 film *Some Came Running*, prepared for prodigal son Dave Hirsh (Frank Sinatra) by his brother Frank (Arthur Kennedy)—but only one because Frank's wife Agnes (Leora Dana) gets "giggly" if she has any more than that. Then of course makeshift Manhattans stole a scene the next year in *Some Like It Hot*, as Marilyn Monroe and Jack Lemmon famously mixed them in a Pullman car, using that hot water bottle as a shaker.

The Manhattan also found its way onto the small screen, too. In "Bart the Murderer"—*The Simpsons*, season 3, episode 4—Bart wipes out on his skateboard in front of the Legitimate Businessman's Social Club, a Mafia

OPPOSITE: *Manhattan Cocktail* movie poster, 1928

MANHATTAN
COCKTAIL

Directed by
DOROTHY ARZNER
Story by
ERNEST VAJDA
Screen play by
ETHEL DOHERTY

WITH
NANCY CARROLL
RICHARD ARLEN
and PAUL LUKAS

a Paramount Picture

front. Some of the members take him in to make sure he's okay, and before you can say Donnie Brasco, Bart becomes one of the goodfellas . . . and their bartender. Ever a quick study, he consults a recipe book and concocts a "*supoib*" drink that one Fat Tony calls one of "the finest Manhattans in Springfield."

Within the pages of literature, the Manhattan appears in countless novels and short stories. In his 1908 short story "The Cop and the Anthem," O. Henry describes a surly New York City waiter as having "a voice like butter cakes and an eye like the cherry in a Manhattan cocktail." In Dashiell Hammett's 1930 noir classic *The Maltese Falcon*, Sam Spade enjoys some bottled Manhattan cocktail from a paper cup, after a long day at the office: "He filled the cup two-thirds full, drank, returned the bottle to the drawer, tossed the cup into the wastebasket, put on his hat and overcoat, turned off the lights, and went down to the night-lit street."

John Dos Passos mentions the drink in *The Big Money*, his 1936 classic, as does Truman Capote in his enduring novella *Breakfast at Tiffany's* (1958). In Jack Kerouac's 1962 novel, *Big Sur*, protagonist Jack Duluoz attempts to escape from fame and civilization by retreating to a rustic cabin in the eponymous California town. He spends time at Nepenthe, then as now "a beautiful cliff top restaurant with vast outdoor patio, with excellent food, excellent waiters and management, good drinks." Among those drinks, Duluoz enjoys the Manhattan—many of them in fact. While "drunk on fifth Manhattan," he expounds to anyone who'll listen (including an army general and lieutenant) his views on guerilla warfare, notably new specialized combat units made up of "dear friends" "all carrying canteens of booze on our belts." Local legend has it that Kerouac became a regular at Nepenthe, knocking back more than a few Manhattans to wash down what he called their "Heavenburgers."

The drink also makes cameos in Irwin Shaw's *Rich Man, Poor Man* (1969) and Kurt Vonnegut's *Breakfast of Champions* (1973).

But let's save our last look at the Manhattan in popular culture for that great 1959 invention: the Cocktailmatic. Why fuss with all that messy measuring and mixing when you could just pop your bottles of whiskey and

OPPOSITE: The Cocktailmatic in action in 1961

vermouth into the handy-dandy Cocktailmatic and, before you know it, a perfect Manhattan dispenses right before your eyes. A 1961 item in the *Lexington Herald-Leader* gives us the skinny:

> Autobar Systems of Sellersville, PA, a division of American Machine & Metal Company, said its new Cocktailmatic machine can do the bartender's work alright—and do it more precisely and with less spillage. They can also keep the bartender honest—Cocktailmatic meters the liquor and records each drink and is locked so nary a drop can be chiseled. . . . But there's no use in going to all that trouble because the bartender still has two vital tasks that no machine could never accomplish. He has to decide whether the customer is old enough to buy a drink legally and make sure he hasn't already had one too many. . . . Then there's the bartender's importance as a social philosopher to be considered. Our bistros just wouldn't seem the same if you had to buy your drinks the way you do from the coffee machines in the office.

The machine sold for the princely sum $365, just shy of $3,000 in today's money when adjusted for inflation. Two years later, the *Trenton Evening Times* waxed even more cynical, questioning the logic of a "dispenser that produces scientifically-proportioned martinis, Manhattans and other cocktails every time. The civilized mind boggles at a contraption which dispenses martinis as the new gasoline pumps choose octane ratings. And what connoisseur worthy of the name wants absolute conformity in the manufacture of his cocktail?"

What connoisseur, indeed? Have you seen one of these contraptions lately?

I didn't think so.

14

A TALE OF TWO CRITICS

"The light music of whisky falling into glasses made an agreeable interlude."

—James Joyce, *Dubliners*

Two seminal works in the field of drink appeared in 1948: *The Hour: A Cocktail Manifesto* by Bernard DeVoto and *The Fine Art of Mixing Drinks* by David Embury. What made these two books different from other bar books already on the market was their authors. Neither man was a bartender. DeVoto was a college professor, historian, and expert on Mark Twain, and he won that year's Pulitzer Prize for history for *Across the Wide Missouri*, a study of the American fur trade in the 1830s. Embury was an attorney and made clear in his own book that he was approaching the topic "entirely as a consumer and as a shaker-upper of drinks." "I am not a distiller, an importer, a bottler, or a merchant of liquors," Embury proclaimed. "I am not even a retired bartender."

Both men had the courage of their opinions—often to the point of cantankerousness, as we'll see. Both books contain part homage, part diatribe. DeVoto offers this morsel of purple prose on cocktail time: "This is the violet hour, the hour of hush and wonder, when the affections glow and the valor is reborn, when the shadows deepen along the edge of the forest and we believe that, if we watch carefully, at any moment we may see the unicorn." The unicorn smacks of a few too many, but the rest is golden.

In DeVoto's estimation, only two cocktails properly existed: a slug of whiskey and the Martini. He howled that "the bar manuals and the women's pages of the daily press . . . print scores of messes to which they give that honorable and glorious name. They are not cocktails. They are slops." He abhorred the Daiquirí, insisting that "No one should drink it

[rum] with a corrosive added, which is the formula of the Daiquiri."

Other memorable DeVotoisms include:

"Throw away that bottle of grenadine. Never buy another one."

"Orange bitters make a good astringent for the face. Never put them in anything that is to be drunk."

"Let's be honest. There is no such thing as a good punch; there isn't even a drinkable one."

DeVoto suffered no patience for those who put olives in martinis and offers a Freudian theory by way of explanation: "presumably because in some desolate childhood hour someone refused them a dill pickle and so they go through life lusting for the taste of brine."

What to do with people garnishing martinis with pickled onion?

"Strangulation seems best."

He insisted that his martinis be made with American gin and in a 3.7:1 ratio of gin to dry vermouth. "It is a grievous betrayal of trust," he said, to use sweet vermouth or a mix of sweet and dry. "Sweet vermouth should not be kept on any shelf in my house or yours; the heathen put it to many uses but we know of none for it."

As such, DeVoto's view on the Manhattan cocktail will come as no shock: "Whiskey and vermouth cannot meet as friends and the Manhattan is an offense against piety. With dry vermouth it is disreputable, with sweet vermouth disgusting. It signifies that the drinker, if male, has no spiritual dignity and would really prefer white mule; if female, a banana split. . . . Let's be clear about this: no Manhattans and no rum."

Embury, who could be just as curmudgeonly as DeVoto, also waxed poetic in his own book. A well-made cocktail

> should stimulate the mind as well as the appetite. The well-made cocktail is one of the most gracious of drinks. It pleases the senses. The shared delight of those who partake in common of this refreshing nectar breaks the ice of formal reserve. Taut nerves relax; taut muscles relax; tired eyes brighten; tongues loosen; friendships deepen; the whole world becomes a better place in which to live.

But he didn't hesitate to train the sharp edge of his tongue on deserving subjects: "It is hard to conceive of any worse cocktail monstrosity than the Vodka Martini, the Vodka Old Fashioned, or Vodka on Rocks." While expounding on the Martini, he noted that "so much of what has been written is pure hooey and balderdash that I cannot refrain from popping off about some of it"—and pop off he did. (Embury even took a few shots at DeVoto: "This gentleman is a facile and highly interesting writer and, except as to gin, rum, and whisky, I have found many of his comments on drinks and drink mixing thoroughly sound. But, when it comes to the Martini, phooey!")

As we saw earlier, Embury gave high marks to the Manhattan, installing it in his own mixological pantheon. In order, he named the pillars of his cocktail temple the Martini, Manhattan, Old-Fashioned, Daiquirí, Sidecar, and Jack Rose. As Embury explains, "I listed the Manhattan second among our six basic cocktails because, of all the hundreds of so-called cocktails listed in recipe books and the dozens listed on the liquor cards of hotels and restaurants, more Martinis and Manhattans are sold than any other kind." He preferred bourbon over rye in his and enjoyed varying the styles of vermouth and bitters and adding a dash of Curaçao or Chartreuse.

= 15 =

POSTWAR VERMOUTH

"Good whiskey was very pleasant. It was one of the pleasant parts of life."

—Ernest Hemingway, *A Farewell to Arms*

Vermouth's exponential growth at the turn of the twentieth century largely derived from the widespread popularity of cocktails like the Manhattan, Martini, and others that incorporated it—but "live by the sword, die by the sword" as the old expression goes. As the second half of the twentieth century swung into view, drinks became drier, and vermouth took a hit. Luminaries such as Winston Churchill and Ernest Hemingway popularized the notion that the drier the Martini, the better. According to popular legend, Churchill only glanced at the bottle of vermouth across the room—or the English Channel—while pouring his measure of gin. In his 1935 light verse poem "A Drink with Something in It," legendary wit Ogden Nash muses on the magic of the Martini, concluding that the delight lies not in the vermouth but the gin.

Cocktail impresario David Embury espoused a 7:1 ratio of gin to vermouth, and by 1955 we see the introduction of a special "atomizer for spraying the merest dash of vermouth into your martinis."

Ernest Hemingway wrote lovingly of vermouth in the 1920s and '30s, but he never wanted much in his Martini. He took umbrage when writer Malcolm Cowley claimed that Hemingway, as a war correspondent, went through World War II with a canteen of gin on one hip and vermouth on the other. Quoth Hemingway: "Can you imagine me wasting a whole canteen on vermouth?" In *Across the River and into the Trees* (1949), Hemingway had given us the Montgomery Martini and its stunning 15:1 gin-to-vermouth ratio, named for Field Marshal Bernard Montgomery, who Hemingway claimed was so cautious that he needed a 15:1 troop superiority before committing them to battle.

Columnist Art Buchwald also took notice. In a tongue-in-cheek piece from July 1957, he discussed the phenomenon.

After World War II, Americans started to insist on drier and drier martinis. State Department officials judged the progress of a country on how dry its martinis had become. No country was doing its share to defeat communism unless the ratio of the martini was five to one. . . . The competition for the American tourist dollar forced the ratio up to six to one, then seven to one, then eight to one. In 1954 the vermouth companies had their blackest year. The ratio at the Crillon Bar, in Paris, the bellwether for dry martinis around the world, had reached 11 to one. Vermouth atomizers were put on the market. Several bartenders bragged they held the vermouth over the shaker without pouring any into the glass. If the ratio reached 12 to one, almost every vermouth company in the world would go out of business.

But in the beginning of 1955 a man at the Ritz Bar, some say it was Ernest Hemingway, told George the bartender, "I want a dry martini, George, but dammit, not too dry." The vermouth companies held their breaths. Whether it was Hemingway or the fact that most countries were on the way to economic recovery and were not as dependent on American aid, the ratio started going down, first 10 to 1, then 9 to 1, then 8 to 1. In 1956 it was down to 6 to 1. And Count Rossi was able to announce at his meeting last week to thunderous applause, that the latest survey showed a wavering between five and six to one. "The worst is over," Count Rossi told his excited audience. "I may be optimistic, but I predict by 1965 that the dry martini may once again be down to three to one. Our factories are prepared to handle the crush."

But just as popular culture brought vermouth along for the merry ride, so it left it at the altar. In 1959's *Some Like It Hot*, as the booze pours into the hot water bottle, one of the women yells, "Hey, easy on the vermouth!" A handful of decades later in *Groundhog Day*, Rita, Andie MacDowell's character, orders a "sweet vermouth on the rocks with a twist." Phil, played by Bill Murray, makes a face—and then grimaces the next day when he orders the same for himself.

According to Anistatia Miller and Jared Brown, "Vermouth has been treated as a necessary evil, when in truth it is the most wrongly maligned beverage behind bars today." They're absolutely right. Until relatively recently, vermouth plain took a beating in popular culture. William Grimes observed: "Martini lore abounds in fanciful ways of rejecting vermouth. It's enough to show the vermouth label to the martini glass, or to 'whisper' vermouth while shaking the drink." In the *Thin Man* films, Nick Charles (played by William Powell) makes a martini with an eyedropper to dispense the vermouth. In the play and movie of *Auntie Mame*, precocious preteen Patrick Dennis makes a martini by rinsing a glass with just a touch of vermouth, then tossing it out. In the 1958 film *Teacher's Pet*, Clark Gable makes his martini by rubbing a cork moistened with vermouth over the rim of the glass.

In an episode of *M*A*S*H*, Alan Alda as Hawkeye Pierce asks the local bartender for "a very dry martini. A very dry, arid, barren, desiccated, veritable dust bowl of a martini. I want a martini that could be declared a disaster area. Mix me just such a martini." In another episode of the same show, Pierce declares that he's hit upon the perfect formula for the dry Martini: Pour the gin while staring at a photo of the inventor of vermouth.

A lead reason for the decline in vermouth's popularity was Prohibition, and vermouth wasn't the only victim. Over the course of those 13 experimental years, Americans simply forgot how to make and drink good cocktails, both in bars and restaurants and at home. The talented craftsmen behind the bar left the country to ply their trade elsewhere—primarily the Caribbean and Europe—while those who stayed behind to man speakeasies hadn't the time, resources, or inclination to make drinks with exotic ingredients. Speakeasies served highballs—whiskey and soda or bathtub gin in an Orange Blossom— not sophisticated cocktails.

The "set-up" became a way of serving drinks so that a saloon could maintain plausible deniability. "Nervous speakeasy owners wanted the option, in case of a raid, of putting the bottles in the overcoat pockets of their customers.

Then they could claim they were only serving set-ups—glasses, ice, and club soda or ginger ale. The set-up quickly became an institution."

Which illustrates that no one had time to sip, savor, and contemplate; it was all too surreptitious. People drank for impact. If you're going to risk fines and imprisonment for each crate of booze coming into your establishment, are you going to waste it, as Hemingway said, on vermouth? Of course not. What you brought in had to have a higher proof.

Imports of vermouth rebounded after Prohibition, but only seven years later World War II threw another monkey wrench in the works. Coming through Italy and southern France, "the flow of imported vermouth from Europe 'slowed down as gradually as an automobile which has smashed into a telephone pole.'" Meanwhile, the American vermouth industry, though growing in size and competency, had come nowhere near where it needed to be to fill the void.

In the 1960s and '70s, parents drank manhattans and martinis. The under-30 set favored highballs—such as the gin or vodka and tonic and the rum or bourbon and Coke®—bloody marys, blender drinks (daiquirís, margaritas, piña coladas), or beer and wine. In other words: drinks that didn't call for vermouth. It became fashionable to disdain such cocktails as old and stuffy. The *Register Star* of Rockford, Illinois, told us in 1981 that it "is now more common to receive an invitation to enjoy wine and cheese over a conversation than it is to be invited to a cocktail party to drink martinis and manhattans." By 1983, the *Dallas Morning News*, in "Take This Test to Find Out How Dull You Are," asked "Do you drink Manhattans?" "Does anyone drink Manhattans today?" *Boston Herald* lifestyle columnist Margery Eagan asked in 1987.

In *The Juice*, Jay McInerney writes of his early fascination with Hemingway and the romance he attached to wine, noting that "The fact that wine had no place on my parents' suburban dining table seemed to confirm its consumption as a mark of sophistication. They and their friends drank cocktails—martinis, Manhattans, old-fashioneds, and stingers. And when they drank enough of them, they behaved badly . . . which didn't strike me as romantic or chic."

Vermouth companies, sensing that their product was becoming a necessary evil, sheepishly marketed themselves accordingly. As vermouth historian

Adam Ford notes:

> Lejon Vermouth, produced in California, touted itself as a vermouth that "knows its place in a martini." So subtle, Lejon prided and preened, it makes a "3:1 taste like a 5:1." The campaign for Cresta, another American brand, exclaimed "At last . . . a White Vermouth created especially for the Dry Martini." It criticized the "pronounced golden color and strong herbal flavor" of traditional dry vermouths, "both American and foreign." Tribuno vermouth, another product blended for American tastes, boasted that it "never overpowers."

Vermouth makers seemed to accept their new role, that they needed to accept a diminished role, to dumb themselves down to play along. Throughout the 1970s and into the 1990s, as younger drinkers stored their bottles of vodka in the freezer to make their drinks as cold as they could be, vermouth fell by the wayside. In the words of Adam Ford: "By 1978, the majority of Americans who bought vermouth were over forty-five years old, and the overwhelming majority of those were women. Hardly anyone under the age of thirty-five ever bought a bottle of vermouth. And so it was for the next thirty years."

By the late 1990s, we saw the start of a renaissance in vermouth itself and classic cocktails in general. In *Straight Up or on the Rocks: The Story of the American Cocktail*, William Grimes surveys the landscape of twentieth-century drinking and carefully chronicles its many peaks and valleys. In closing one of the chapters, he correctly predicts: "The new millennium has barely begun to take its first, halting steps, but for the cocktail the immediate future looks very bright. More than a century after the martini and the Manhattan conquered the world, the American mixed drink looks poised to enter its second golden age."

Truer words were never spoken. In the late 1990s the beginnings of the cocktail renaissance emerged, with its emphasis on quality spirits, authentic recipes, fresh juices, and classic techniques. Which brings us back to the resurgence in vermouth. Not only was the cocktail world ready for its reemergence, so was vermouth. In the words of Eric Seed, owner of Haus Alpenz—importer and distributor of Cocchi® Americano, Cocchi Vermouth di Torino, Dolin Vermouth, St. Elizabeth™ Allspice Dram, and other offerings—"It's a testament to the cocktail revival that we again have qualities of vermouth that enable the Manhattan to work at 1:1 proportions. We also see a growing customer base that looks for specific styles of vermouth well beyond the simplistic (and largely unhelpful) labels of 'Italian vs. French,' or 'dry vs. sweet.'"

Giuseppe Gallo, global brand ambassador for Martini & Rossi, notes that "In the last four to five years we have seen a resurgence in the vermouth category mainly driven by bartenders focusing more on classic cocktails, where the vermouth is (and has been always) a major cocktail ingredient." All vermouth brands are seeing higher volume growth in the bars and restaurants category in the United Kingdom (24 percent), and in the United States (6 percent) largely due to the cocktail renaissance. That upward trend in sales and use eventually translates into higher sales and use by consumers.

As Adam Ford puts it:

In 2009 there were no modern American vermouth producers. In 2012 there were three. Now there are dozens of companies commercially producing vermouth in the United States, with dozens more working to perfect their formulas. . . . It is particularly fascinating that for the past 200 years vermouth has been produced essentially the same way, resulting in vermouths with minimal flavor differences other than the split between dry and sweet. Today, however, American producers are making vermouths that taste nothing like one another and nothing like their European counterparts.

As you will see from the recipes in the next part of this book, which span more than a century, the Manhattan isn't going anywhere. It's here to stay. Today's top craft bartenders are experimenting with the original Manhattan, as well as its descendants, with great frequency and greater success. Let's raise our glasses to that.

= 16 =

INNOVATION

*"The heat of day lingered in the blue and white blocks of the
balcony, and from the great canvas mats our friends had
spread along the terrace we warmed our sunburned backs and
invented new cocktails."*

—F. Scott Fitzgerald, *The Jazz Age*

f you can master the sour cocktail, you can use it as an agile basis for
inventing numerous new drinks. If you can find the right balance between
sweet (such as simple syrup, triple sec, orange Curaçao), strong (rum,
whiskey, tequila, etc.), and sour (lemon or lime juice), you can have a lot of
fun making new cocktails by swapping options. The same holds true for the
Manhattan. As DC bartender and bar owner Derek Brown puts it:

> When I first starting bartending, this was the only drink I saw
> bartenders take time to try and construct thoughtfully. . . . It was a
> point of pride. People doused the rim with cherry juice, rubbed a
> piece of lemon on it, swore that a little bit of Maraschino liqueur was
> the key. While all of these seem throw backs now, this was a lot more
> effort than they'd put into any other drink and with little complaint.
>
> That doesn't mean it was without its misinterpretation and
> degradation. I worked at a restaurant called Palena that had a group
> of, shall we say, old-school waiters. The kind who knew how to make
> bananas flambés table-side. One of the waiters was named Guy. He
> was French. I made him a Manhattan, 2:1, with a dash of bitters, for
> a guest (my preferred recipe to this day). He swore up and down that
> bitters were a mistake. I disagreed. After I brought an old book with
> the recipe spelled out, he admitted that it was because customers don't
> like bitters. I asked the customers how they liked it. They said it was

the best they'd ever had. It was then that I realized just how much things were going to change.

Take a look at the Brooklyn recipe chapter (page 205) as well as the other contemporary takes on the Manhattan. What's the common denominator? Like the sour, you have that basic three-part structure: sweet, bitter, and strong. In the Greenpoint, sweet vermouth shares space with Chartreuse. In the Red Hook, maraschino complements the other flavors. In the Little Italy, it's Cynar®. In the Copperhead, apple brandy takes the place of whiskey, and the delightful Cocchi Barolo Chinato adds both bitter and honey notes. As David Embury suggested in 1948, you can use these components to "roll your own"—that is, to create new drinks. He did just that by adding Byrrh® to the Manhattan to create the delicious Marianne (page 175).

Following that directive will allow you to engage in a little creativity and introduce you to new flavors. Apéritif bitters, including Aperol®, Campari, and Cynar, await, as do amari such as Byrrh, Cardamaro®, Cocchi Americano Rosa, Cocchi Barolo Chinato, Rabarbaro Zucca® and Swedish punsch. Liqueurs and spirits such as absinthe, Bénédictine®, Chartreuse, parfait amour, sherry, and a range of other amazing products also stand ready to serve.

As I've noted before, we're seeing a renaissance in vermouth, with new offerings both imported and domestic. Martini has launched a new Riserva Speciale line (the Rubino and Ambrato are delicious), and we're seeing new domestic brands, such as Atsby®, Capitoline, Uncouth®, and Vya®.

Ten years ago you might have found one or two ryes and no applejack on the shelves of your local liquor store, but now is an amazing time to try different spirits. The choice is staggering. Small distilleries are popping up all over the country. Excellent new whiskeys are coming from countries such as Japan and France, and we're seeing vast improvements in whiskeys from Canada, notably premium brands, such as Caribou Crossing™ (from Sazerac Co.), that are redefining this much-maligned category. Not all of these new creations will work, but you'll develop a better palate and appreciation for their flavors.

PART TWO

THE DRINKS

= RECIPES =

"I'd like to be sitting with Samuel Clemens, Groucho
Marx, Mae West, and W. C. Fields drinking Manhattans
and listening to Louis Armstrong live while we place our
bets on the Kentucky Derby."

—Dale DeGroff, as quoted in *The 12 Bottle Bar*

n 1898, the author of Livermore & Knight's *Cocktails: How to Make Them*, put it succinctly· "the addition of Vermouth was the first move toward the blending of cocktails and was the initial feature that led to their popularity." When bartenders discovered the magic of vermouth, they threw open the doors to innovation. In other words, the Manhattan has launched a thousand ships.

What follows are some of the world's best cocktails built on the Manhattan's spirit-vermouth-bitters platform, beginning with timeless iterations of the Manhattan proper, a range of pre–World War II drinks inspired by it, and then contemporary takes from around the world. In the following pages, I've made a number of recommendations as to brands of whiskey, vermouth, and other ingredients, but every palate is different, so feel free to use your own favorites instead of mine.

Also, as we saw in the first part of the book, the creation date of a particular recipe isn't necessarily the same as when it first appears in print, and sometimes later versions are more noteworthy. The following recipes loosely proceed in chronological order as an organizing principle, which demonstrates, in the big picture, how the Manhattan evolved before, during, and after Prohibition. (For cocktail fanatics, a more extensive and also chronological table of pre-Prohibition recipes follows in the appendix.)

Finally, as mentioned at the end of Chapter 6—and it's worth repeating—don't ruin your Manhattans or any other cocktail with those dyed cherry monsters in the canned-fruit aisle of your grocery store.

THE THREE CLASSIC

MANHATTANS

Traditional Manhattan

2 ounces bourbon or rye whiskey
1 ounce sweet vermouth
2 dashes aromatic bitters
   lemon peel or cherry for garnish

In a mixing glass, stir all ingredients with large ice cubes, strain into a chilled cocktail glass, and garnish with a lemon peel or a cocktail cherry.

Dry Manhattan

2 ounces bourbon or rye whiskey
1 ounce dry vermouth
2 dashes aromatic bitters
   lemon peel or cherry for garnish

In a mixing glass, stir all ingredients with large ice cubes, strain into a chilled cocktail glass, and garnish with a lemon peel or a cocktail cherry.

Perfect Manhattan

2 ounces bourbon or rye whiskey
½ ounce dry vermouth
½ ounce sweet vermouth
2 dashes aromatic bitters
   lemon peel or cherry for garnish

In a mixing glass, stir all ingredients with large ice cubes, strain into a chilled cocktail glass, and garnish with a lemon peel or a cocktail cherry.

18

MANHATTAN-INSPIRED COCKTAILS FROM

THE MANHATTAN CLUB,

CIRCA 1893

The cocktails in this next section all appear in an 1893 article on the history of the Manhattan Club that ran in *New York Sun*, which boasted that "More famous drinks have been invented at the Manhattan than at any other place in the country." Most of these drinks contain equal parts vermouth to spirits—as is the case with the recipe for the Manhattan in that same article—or 2:1 in favor of vermouth. Reading a vintage recipe and drinking a cocktail made from one are different experiences, so feel free to play around with the proportions to taste.

LEFT: The A. T. Stewart Mansion, on the northwest corner of 34th and Fifth, stood across the street from where the Empire State Building stands today and was home to the Manhattan Club in the 1890s.

Manhattan Cocktail à la Gilbert

D avid B. Gilbert, familiarly known as "Uncle Dave," was called the "Watchdog" of the Manhattan Club, which he joined in 1882. Called "perhaps the most striking personality ever on the Manhattan Club's roster," Gilbert was the club's secretary for 17 years and a prominent member of the New York Stock Exchange. "It would be difficult to parallel the intense love and devotion— almost religious in its fervor . . . which he displayed, every moment of his life, towards the advancement of the best interests of the Club." As we've seen, this drink makes the connection between the Manhattan and the traditional Brooklyn (page 145) with minor adjustments to the representations of whiskey and vermouth.

> 1½ ounces bourbon or rye (such as Russell's Reserve®
> 10-year-old bourbon or 6-year-old rye)
> 1½ ounces Martini dry vermouth
> 1 dash Amer Picon bitters
> lemon peel or cherry for garnish

Stir well with ice, strain into a chilled cocktail glass, and garnish with a lemon peel or a cocktail cherry.

NOTE

In this and other cocktail books, a number of drinks call for Amer Picon, an apéritif bitter from France that is fairly impossible to find in America and, like other iconic brands (Coca-Cola®, Bacardi, Gordon's® gin, and Kina Lillet for example), recently underwent a change in formula. Many sources advise using Torani® Amer instead, but purists will say it's just not the same—nor is it easy to find, either. Other alternatives embraced by the craft bartending community include Amaro CioCiaro®; Amaro Ramazzotti® seasoned further with Angostura® Orange Bitters; Amer Boudreau, a concoction perfected by Jamie Boudreau of the bar Canon in Seattle, consisting of Ramazzotti, Stirrings® Blood Orange Bitters, orange tincture (dried orange peels steeped in vodka), and Evian® spring water (recipe here: https:// spiritsandcocktails.wordpress.com/2007/09/09/amer-picon); or Bigallet China-China amer.

The Plimpton Cocktail

Think of this as the original rum Manhattan. After the *New York Sun* article, you'll find it again in the pages both of Grohusko's *Jack's Manual* and Jacques Straub's 1914 *Drinks*. It's nearly identical to the Palmetto, found below, but for the different bitters. As for the origin of the name, that's a bit of a head-scratcher. The Plimpton name has a longstanding connection to New York City. A prominent Manhattan resident named George A. Plimpton, who had graduated from Phillips Exeter Academy, belonged to a number of associations and societies, including the Delta Kappa Epsilon Club, but he appears to have no connection to the Manhattan Club or the drink. Barnard College in uptown Manhattan has a Plimpton Hall, and a popular nineteenth-century meeting venue had that same name. (Horace Greeley spoke there in 1872.) Across the Harlem River, the Bronx has a Plimpton Avenue. But no other information helps identify the source of the name. Nevertheless, this is a delicious cocktail, and that might be all you need to know.

> 2 ounces Appleton® Estate Reserve Blend Jamaican rum
> 1 ounce Carpano Antica Formula® sweet vermouth
> 2 dashes Angostura bitters
>   lemon peel or cherry for garnish

Stir well with ice, strain into a chilled cocktail glass, and garnish with a lemon peel or a cocktail cherry.

Queen Anne Cocktail

The *New York Sun* described this drink as "made of brandy, vermouth, orange bitters and maraschino"—but of course no volumes or ratios. I've created an interpretation that I believe works nicely, but feel free to adjust to taste. In 1705, Anne, queen of England, Scotland, and Ireland, granted 215 acres of farmland in lower Manhattan to Trinity Church. (In the two centuries since, the church has divested itself of most of that original land grant.) Two years later, she led an alliance of the newly created nation of Britain, the Holy Roman Empire, and Holland against France's King Louis XIV in the War of Spanish Succession, thereby maintaining Europe's tenuous balance of power. So here's to Good Queen Anne!

> 2 ounces Pierre Ferrand® 1840 Original Formula Cognac
> 1 ounce La Quintinye Extra Dry Vermouth
> 1 dash Regans'® Orange Bitters No. 6
> 1 dash Luxardo maraschino liqueur
> lemon peel or cherry for garnish

Stir well with ice, strain into a chilled cocktail glass, and garnish with a lemon peel or a cocktail cherry.

NOTE

This isn't the only Queen Anne Cocktail that you'll find in print. In his must-have book, *Vintage Spirits and Forgotten Cocktails*, my friend Ted Haigh notes that by adding peach bitters to an Algonquin (page 153) you get a different Queen Anne.

Smithtown Cocktail

W e don't know much about this drink, which is a shame. Presumably it takes its name from the town in Suffolk County on Long Island, but even that's not clear. It appears in the 1893 *New York Sun* story and again in *The History of the Manhattan Club*, published in 1915 on the club's fiftieth anniversary, but mysteriously it doesn't turn up in any of the bar guides of the day. It's one of the earliest drinks to introduce citrus into the Manhattan platform—essentially the Whiskey Sour meets the Dry Manhattan—which eventually led to drinks such as the El Presidente. Substitute orange bitters for grenadine, and you get the Scofflaw (page 163).

 2 ounces Redemption Rye Whiskey
 1 ounce Carpano extra dry vermouth
 ½ ounce fresh lemon juice
 1 dash Fee Brothers orange bitters
 lemon peel or cherry for garnish

Shake with ice, strain into a chilled cocktail glass, and garnish with a lemon peel or a cocktail cherry.

The Star Cocktail

The *New York Sun* article simply states that this drink consists "of applejack, vermouth, yellow Chartreuse and cherry bounce." It was fairly popular in the 1890s: You'll find it in the "Leading Barkeeper's Report" (*Evansville Courier*, November 6, 1894), and the *Cincinnati Post* of October 20, 1897, quoted bartender G. J. Prell of the Gibson bar as saying that "the very latest thing is the 'star' cocktail." But the recipe, like so many drinks of the time, was a moving target. Harry Johnson's 1888 *Bartender's Manual* called for gum syrup, Curaçao, Boker's bitters, applejack, and vermouth. George Kappeler offered his rendering in *Modern American Drinks* (1895), in which he included Peychaud's bitters—but no mention of cherry bounce or Chartreuse. G. J. Prell noted that "It is made of apple brandy, vermouth and orange bitters." Grohusko's classic *Jack's Manual* (1908) reverts back to the Prell recipe. This version remains true to the 1893 *New York Sun* recitation:

> 1½ ounce Laird's® Straight Apple Brandy
> 1½ ounce Martini sweet vermouth
> 1 teaspoon Cherry Heering
> ½ teaspoon yellow Chartreuse
> 1 dash Peychaud's bitters
> lemon peel or cherry for garnish

Stir well with ice, strain into a chilled cocktail glass, and garnish with a lemon peel or a cocktail cherry.

NOTE

If you can't find Laird's Straight Apple Brandy, you can use Laird's AppleJack, but the brandy is better. The bitters are optional, but, again, the drink is better with them. Cherry bounce is an infusion of cherries, sugar, and brandy, rum, or whiskey, but you're more likely to find Cherry Heering at your local store.

19

PRE-WORLD WAR II DRINKS
BASED ON THE
MANHATTAN
FORMULA

According to my friends Gary Regan and Mardee Haidin Regan, "The way we see it: The Manhattan spawned the Martinez, which sired the Martini, which evolved into the Dry Martini." With brevity comes tranquility, so I'll leave it at that. Countless cocktails have poured forth from the immortal combination of gin and vermouth—from the Marguerite and the Montgomery to the Vesper and the Obituary. The list goes on. As such, I'll start this chapter by offering just a trio of gin-based drinks, keeping in mind that this is a book about the Manhattan, not the Martini. (Nor will I stir up the tempest in a teapot of the relationship between the Martinez and Martini.)

The Martinez

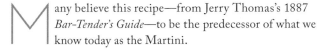

M any believe this recipe—from Jerry Thomas's 1887 *Bar-Tender's Guide*—to be the predecessor of what we know today as the Martini.

1 ounce Hayman's™ Old Tom gin
3 ounces Dolin Rouge sweet vermouth
2 dashes maraschino liqueur
2 dashes gum or simple syrup (optional, to taste)
1 dash Adam Elmegirab's Boker's Bitters
lemon peel for garnish

Shake with ice, strain into a large chilled cocktail glass, and garnish with a quarter slice of lemon.

The Marguerite

F irst seen in Harry Johnson's 1900 edition of *Bartenders' Manual*, this recipe gives us the combination of an English dry gin, dry vermouth, and orange bitters—as opposed to the sweeter gin, vermouth, and bitters found in most Martini and Martinez recipes of the day. Many cocktail historians, including yours truly, count this as the forefather of the Dry Martini. Enjoy it while recalling that great line from George Burns: "Happiness is a dry Martini and a good woman . . . or a bad woman."

1½ ounces Plymouth gin
1½ ounces Noilly Prat dry vermouth
2 or 3 dashes of anisette
2 or 3 dashes of orange bitters
lemon peel
cherry for garnish

In a mixing glass filled with crushed ice, stir all ingredients well, and strain into a chilled cocktail glass. Twist a piece of lemon peel over the top, and discard. Garnish with a cocktail cherry.

The Martini

When the Martini first came along, this recipe—from Harry Johnson's 1888 *Bartenders' Manual*—is how it was made. Note the sweeter style of gin, sweet vermouth, and even more sweetness from the gum syrup.

    1½ ounces Hayman's Old Tom gin
    1½ ounces Dolin Rouge sweet vermouth
    2 or 3 dashes gum or simple syrup
    2 or 3 dashes Adam Elmegirab's Boker's Bitters
    cherry or olive for garnish
    lemon peel for garnish

In a mixing glass filled with ice, stir all ingredients well. Strain into a cocktail glass, and garnish with a cocktail cherry or medium-sized olive. Twist a piece of lemon peel over the top, and discard.

Metropolitan

Opened in 1852, the Metropolitan Hotel stood at the corner of Broadway and Prince Street. Jerry Thomas worked there from 1858 to 1860, although this drink likely came along later—after 1880. Found in O. H. Byron's 1884 *Modern Bartenders' Guide*, the original recipe called for French (meaning: dry) vermouth. Later iterations of the recipe, such as the one that appears in the *Old Waldorf-Astoria Bar Book*, call for sweet vermouth, which I recommend. The hotel was demolished in 1895.

½ ounce Pierre Ferrand 1840 Original Formula Cognac or other brandy

1 ounce Martini sweet vermouth

3 dashes Angostura bitters

3 dashes gum or simple syrup (optional, to taste)

lemon peel or cherry for garnish

Stir well with ice, strain into a chilled cocktail glass, and garnish with a lemon peel or a cocktail cherry.

NOTE

Not to be confused with the above, the Metropole is a similar drink but calls for dry vermouth and a combination of Peychaud's and orange bitters.

Saratoga Cocktail

Named for the famous resort town of Saratoga Springs, New York—a popular destination for the elite and sporting classes of the Gilded Age—this recipe first appeared in Jerry Thomas's 1887 *Bar-Tender's Guide*, which presented an entire suite of Saratoga drinks: the Saratoga Cocktail, Saratoga Pousse Café, Saratoga Brace-Up, and Saratoga Cooler. (The latter three have rather sweet flavor profiles, so this is the one of the bunch that you'll want to drink.)

    1 ounce Pierre Ferrand 1840 Original Formula Cognac
      or other brandy
    1 ounce Wild Turkey® 101 bourbon or rye whiskey
    1 ounce Carpano Antica Formula sweet vermouth
    2 dashes Angostura bitters
      lemon peel for garnish

Shake well with ice, strain into a chilled cocktail glass, and serve with a quarter of a slice of lemon.

NOTE

This drink may well be the inspiration for the acclaimed Vieux Carré Cocktail (page 166).

Rob Roy

The name of this drink honors the Reginald de Koven operetta that opened in New York City in 1894 and, by association, Scottish national hero Rob Roy McGregor. In *Everyday Drinking*, Kingsley Amis notes that although "Bourbon whiskey blends into cocktails . . . Scotch stands apart, proudly resistant to being combined with fruit juice, bitters, vermouth . . . almost anything." Not many cocktails contain Scotch, but this one does, and it's a classic. As David Wondrich notes of that era's Scotch cocktails: "the only one of them to gain any traction was the Rob Roy, which was the first of them all and is still going strong." This recipe hails from Jacques Straub's *Drinks* (1914).

   2 ounces Monkey Shoulder® Scotch whisky
   1 ounce Dolin Rouge sweet vermouth
   1 dash Regans' Orange Bitters No. 6
   1 dash Angostura or Fee Brothers aromatic bitters
   lemon peel or cherry for garnish

Stir well with ice, strain into a chilled cocktail glass, and garnish with a lemon peel or a cocktail cherry.

NOTE

If this recipe strikes your Scottish fancy, consider its spinoffs: the Robert Burns (Scotch, sweet vermouth, orange bitters, absinthe), Bobby Burns (Scotch, sweet vermouth, Bénédictine), and the Tale of Two Roberts (page 191). Also have a look at Hugo Ensslin's 1916 classic, the Affinity (Scotch, sweet and dry vermouth, Angostura bitters).

Fanciulli Cocktail

S ucceeding the illustrious John Philip Sousa in 1892, Francesco Fanciulli was the director of the U.S. Marine Band. But an unfortunate incident during the 1897 Memorial Day parade interrupted Fanciulli's career. Lt. T. L. Draper wanted the band to play "music with swing to it," namely a Sousa ditty called "El Capitan." Fanciulli told Draper to pound sand. Lt. Draper firmly replied: "You'll play what I order you to play." Ultimately, "the lieutenant ordered him to return at once to the marine barracks and report himself under arrest to the officer in charge." Publicly disgraced, Fanciulli later was court martialed and convicted, but he appealed his case to the assistant secretary of the Navy, a bespectacled fellow named Theodore Roosevelt, who overturned the verdict. Bully for Fanciulli!

 2 ounces Buffalo Trace™ bourbon
 1 ounce Carpano Antica Formula vermouth
 ¼ ounce Fernet-Branca®
 lemon peel for garnish

Stir well with ice, strain into a chilled cocktail glass, and garnish with a lemon peel.

NOTE
You also can serve the drink over ice in a rocks glass.

FANCIULLI UNDER ARREST

Leader of the Marine Band
Charged With Insubordination.

Ordered From the Head of the Parade Today
and Directed to Report at the Barracks.

There was but one unpleasant incident connected with today's parade, and that resulted in the technical arrest of Prof. F. Fanciulli, leader of the Marine Band, which band headed the line and subsequently took part in the ceremonies at Arlington. It occurred while the line was forming on the north side of Pennsylvania avenue, and the band stood at rest just above Willard's Hotel, awaiting the signal to start. The arrest was due to a disagreement between Prof. Fanciulli and Lieut. T. L. Draper of the United States Marine Corps, commanding the marine contingent of the parade, concerning the character of the music furnished.

From the *Washington Evening Star*, May 31, 1897

More than a decade later, when former president Roosevelt returned from a trip abroad, a "monster reception" greeted him. Initially the reception committee hired Fanciulli's band to play at the event, but the committee learned that the New York City Musical Union had suspended the band leader for failure to pay his musicians. As a result, the committee gave the gig to another group and offered Fanciulli a $25 settlement. Through his attorney, he countered that, since "it was impossible to estimate the damage," he opted to "leave it for a jury to decide." What did the spurned Fanciulli do? He sued the committee for $50,000! It's unclear how he fared in court, but clearly the Tuscan native had fully acclimated to life in America.

Bronx Cocktail

P opular from its inception, circa 1900, until the start of World War II, the Bronx Cocktail more or less disappeared thereafter. Only in the last decade has it experienced a resurgence. In F. Scott Fitzgerald's *This Side of Paradise* (1920), protagonist Amory Blaine tosses back more than a few at the Knickerbocker Hotel to forget the pain of a bad breakup, "his head spinning gorgeously, layer upon layer of soft satisfaction setting over the bruised spots of his spirit." The Bronx was also Bill Wilson's first drink. He called it "wonderful, sweet and airy at the same time. . . . My gaucheries and ineptitudes magically disappeared. . . . I had found the elixir of life." Who is Bill Wilson, you ask? He founded Alcoholics Anonymous, so be careful of this one, folks!

> 1½ ounces Fords Gin® or other London dry gin
> ½ ounce Dolin dry vermouth
> ½ ounce Dolin Rouge sweet vermouth
> ½ ounce orange juice

Shake over ice, and strain into a chilled cocktail glass. No garnish.

Succasuma Cocktail

This drink appears in the pages of the May 8, 1904, edition of the *New York Times* in a column called "SPRING FASHIONS IN DRINKS; Just as New Clothes Come Into Vogue. So Do Strange Beverages Appear in the Cafes of New York." The story notes that "Another one new to Broadway is known as the 'Succasuma Cocktail,' and is made up of applejack, vermouth, and a dash of Angostura bitters." The origin of the drink and its name is unclear. The name might stem from names of towns in New York or New Jersey (both alternatively spelled "Succasunna" in modern directories). In any event, this delicious cocktail is worthy of a greater share of the spotlight more than a century after its debut. Here's how.

 2 ounces Laird's Straight Apple Brandy or Laird's AppleJack
 1 ounce Dolin Rouge sweet vermouth
 2 dashes Angostura bitters

Stir well with ice, and strain into a chilled cocktail glass. No garnish.

Blackthorn (Irish Variation)

The Blackthorn has several variations. I dare not offer you the version made with sloe gin, sweet and dry vermouth, and Peychaud's and orange bitters. Why not? Because the *Los Angeles Herald* of December 13, 1905, tells of a fellow, drunk on that other variant, who claimed that for three days he "roamed in a region of imaginary monsters of the most horrible sizes, shapes and hues" and that "children playing in the streets looked like differently colored overgrown toads, some with large heads of animals and some with heads and hands almost invisible." Best to avoid that one, but the Irish version is safe.

> 1 ounce Tullamore D.E.W.™ Irish whiskey
> 1 ounce Martini sweet vermouth
> ¼ ounce absinthe or Herbsaint
> 3 dashes Angostura bitters

Stir well with ice, and strain into a chilled cocktail glass. No garnish, and *sláinte!*

NOTE

On March 18, 1905, the *New York Times* tells of a similar drink made by an Irish bartender at the Hotel Netherland. He interrupted the St. Patrick's Day parade the day prior by insisting that marchers from the Sixty-ninth Regiment take "Shamrock cocktails." When asked what they contained, he replied "Just a little Irish whisky, some French vermouth, and a dash of Orange bitters." According to the *Times*, "Quiet was restored when the bitters were omitted."

Brooklyn Cocktail

The earliest known (and likely best) recipe for the Brooklyn goes back to 1908, found in J. A. "Jack" Grohusko's classic *Jack's Manual: On the Vintage and Production, Care, and Handling of Wines, Liquors, Etc.* Today's traditional recipe uses dry vermouth, but this one calls for sweet, resulting in a superior drink. This is a delightful variation on the Manhattan, but the trick to making it is to find a worthy substitute for the elusive Amer Picon.

> 1½ ounces Wild Turkey 101 rye whiskey
> 1½ ounces Carpano Antica Formula sweet vermouth
> 1 dash Amer Picon bitters
> 1 dash Luxardo or Leopold Bros. maraschino liqueur

Stir well with ice, and strain into a chilled cocktail glass.

NOTE

See page 123 for options to replace the Amer Picon above, and also chapters 11 and 22 for the history and further recipe variations.

Palmetto Cocktail

n April 1892, the *New York Sun* ran a short piece concerning William "the Only William" Schmidt. A customer had ordered a Manhattan during Holy Week, which Schmidt considered uncouth. "What you probably would prefer, sir, is a Palmetto cocktail," he advised, describing it as "a nectar fit for the gods." The customer inquired as to the ingredients, and Schmidt replied: "That, sir, is a secret of the profession." A week later, James J. Hayes wrote to the editor, challenging Schmidt's inventorship. "As manager of the French Café I dispute his claim, having made the 'Palmetto' spoken of for the last year and a half," adding pointedly that "I am the only and original man who mixed this delightful concoction." Another week on, Schmidt observed that "Name is one thing and composition is another. Why did said Mr. J.J.H. not publish his recipe, that another man in the line can find out; but heaven may know what may be in it. I think that palmetto taken at Christmas is rather out of season, and this is the only way I can figure up his year and a half. Had he said a year or two or three now, he might be right, but palmetto begins with Palm Sunday and ends with Easter Sunday, so there can be no palmetto during the rest of the year." Schmidt closed with, "Would like to hear if my opponent took out a copyright for the title; if so, I am willing to refund his expenses." Hayes made no return volley. An early if not the earliest appearance of the recipe comes from J. A. Grohusko's 1908 *Jack's Manual* and calls for equal parts rum to vermouth, but the 2:1 ratio below offers better balance. Grohusko specifies Angostura bitters, but the *Savoy Cocktail Book* calls for orange bitters. They both work, so you decide.

> 2 ounces Papa's Pilar® dark rum
> 1 ounce Martini sweet vermouth
> 2 dashes Regans' Orange Bitters No. 6 or
> Angostura bitters
> lemon peel for garnish

Stir well with ice, strain into a chilled cocktail glass, and garnish with a lemon peel.

Bwano Tumbo

F ollowing his presidency, Theodore Roosevelt traveled extensively around the world. In 1910, he toured the wilds of Africa, where he went on many a safari. The natives there came to call him Bwano Tumbo, which in Swahili means "portly master." This drink, created to celebrate his homecoming, contains ingredients representing five nations—plus another for the serving glass—in honor of TR's global excursions.

¾ ounce San Juan rum (Cuba)
⅜ ounce dry gin (England)
⅜ ounce sweet vermouth (Italy)
1 dash absinthe (France)
1 dash kirschwasser (Germany)

Stir well with ice, and strain into a chilled Venetian (Austrian) glass. No garnish.

NOTE

Napoleon Bonaparte conquered Venice in 1797 and ceded it to the archduchy of Austria, within the Holy Roman Empire, but then reclaimed it for the kingdom of Italy in 1805. After Bonaparte's 1814 defeat, Venice became part of the Austrian-controlled kingdom of Lombardy before returning to the kingdom of Italy in 1866. All of which is to say that, if you don't have Venetian glasses handy, you can substitute a regular cocktail glass.

Harvard Cocktail

I n years past, many of the Ivy League schools had their own signature cocktails. For example, the Princeton consists of Old Tom gin, orange bitters, and port—a tad sweet, but the Tigers liked it. The recipe for Harvard's—from the 1912 *Wehman Brothers Bartender's Guide*—is one of the more palatable. *Ad veritatem!*

> 1½ ounces Pierre Ferrand 1840 Original Formula Cognac
> 1½ ounces Carpano Antica Formula sweet vermouth
> 3 dashes Adam Elmegirab's Boker's Bitters
> lemon peel for garnish

Stir well with ice, strain into a chilled cocktail glass, and garnish with a lemon peel.

OPPOSITE: Johnston Gate opening onto Harvard Yard in 1899

Deshler

Hugo Ensslin tended the bar at the Hotel Wallick in Times Square and was asked to create a new drink for a sister hotel, the Deshler-Wallick in Columbus, Ohio. This brilliant result first appeared in his legendary self-published bar guide, *Recipes for Mixed Drinks* (1916).

    1½ ounces Wild Turkey 101 rye whiskey
    1 ounce Dubonnet® rouge
    ¼ ounce Cointreau
    2 orange peels, plus one for garnish
    1 lemon peel

Stir all ingredients (including two orange peels and the lemon peel) well with ice, strain into a chilled cocktail glass, and garnish with the third orange peel.

Creole Cocktail

This recipe also hails from Hugo Ensslin's *Recipes for Mixed Drinks*, perhaps the last major cocktail manual before Prohibition began. The term *creole* has many connotations and definitions, and much depends on the historical and cultural context: who used the word when. In the eighteenth and nineteenth centuries, *créole* referred to the children of Spanish or French emigrants to the New World, such as the Creoles of Louisiana. In other words, the parents were born in the Old Country, came to America, and their children were creoles. Over time, the term came to apply to people of color who also could trace their ancestry back to Europe. In the twentieth and twenty-first centuries, *creole* more likely refers to a person of mixed African and French or Spanish heritage. Within the black community in Louisiana, the use of lower or upper case *C* can imply social standing. It's complicated—but fortunately the drink isn't!

> 1½ ounce Sazerac® rye
> 1½ ounce Martini sweet vermouth
> 2 dashes Amer Picon
> 2 dashes Bénédictine

Stir well with ice, strain into a chilled cocktail glass, garnish with either a lemon peel or a cocktail cherry.

NOTE
See page 123 for options to replace the elusive Amer Picon above.

Algonquin

The Algonquin Hotel stands at 59 West 44th Street in Manhattan's Club Row. In June 1919, two Broadway publicists hosted a lunchtime roast for drama critic Alexander Woollcott there, and it soon became the ongoing meeting place for a collection of actors, critics, editors, journalists, and other writers who (eventually) gathered around a round table and attracted the sobriquet of the "Vicious Circle." Notable members included Franklin P. Adams, Robert Benchley, Edna Ferber, George Kaufman, Harpo Marx, Dorothy Parker, Harold Ross, Robert Sherwood, Peggy Wood, and of course Alexander Woollcott. The hotel serves this cocktail in their honor.

> 1½ ounces Sazerac rye whiskey
> ¾ ounce Martini dry vermouth
> ¾ ounce unsweetened pineapple juice
> cherry for garnish

Stir well with ice, and strain into a chilled cocktail glass or an ice-filled rocks glass. Garnish with a cocktail cherry.

NOTE

If you find this drink a touch dry, add a dash or two of simple syrup to taste.

Blood & Sand

This classic takes its name from the 1922 silent film starring Rudolph Valentino (né Rodolfo Guglielmi). In his classic book, *The Craft of the Cocktail*, my friend and mentor Dale DeGroff, the King of Cocktails, perfectly expresses the sentiments that many have held about this drink: "At first glance, this unusual cocktail seemed a godawful mix. But over time, I noted that the recipe appeared in some serious cocktail books, so I finally tried it. The taste convinced me never to judge a drink again without tasting it." All hail the king!

> ¾ ounce Monkey Shoulder Scotch whisky
> ¾ ounce Cherry Heering
> ¾ ounce Martini sweet vermouth
> 1 ounce orange juice
> orange for garnish

Shake well with ice, strain into a chilled cocktail glass, and garnish with a flamed orange peel.

JESSE L. LASKY
presents

Rodolph Valentino

IN

a FRED NIBLO Production

BLOOD AND SAND

SUPPORTED BY

LILA LEE and NITA NALDI

▼

A Paramount Picture

El Presidente

The namesake of this drink is Mario García Menocal y Deop, second president of Cuba's second republic, who served from 1913 to 1921—and that's where the historical consensus ends. A number of Cuban bars claim credit for creating this cocktail. According to tiki expert Jeff "Beachbum" Berry, the drink originally appeared in the 1924 *Manual del Cantinero*. Cocktail historian and *Wall Street Journal* columnist Eric Felten says the drink debuted at the Vista Alegre Club in Santiago de Cuba. David Wondrich credits the drink to Constantino "El Constante" Ribalaigua i Vert, owner and barman of the legendary Bar la Florida, now known as El Floridita. Now, that's the sort of presidential debate I can get my hands around. Make yourself one, and you decide.

    1 ounce añejo Cuban rum
    2 ounces Dolin Vermouth de Chambéry Blanc
    ¼ ounce Pierre Ferrand dry Curaçao
    ½ teaspoon grenadine
    1 dash Angostura bitters
    1 orange peel
    cherry for garnish

Add all liquid ingredients to a mixing glass filled with ice. Twist the orange peel over the top, and drop it in. Stir well for at least 30 seconds. Strain into a chilled cocktail glass, and garnish with a cocktail cherry.

NOTE

If Cuban rum is unavailable, Berry suggests Banks 7 Golden Age Rum® blend or Cruzan® Single Barrel rum. Wondrich suggests Banks 5 Island®.

The 2-to-1 ratio of vermouth to rum comes from the first printed version of the recipe, which appears in the 1915 edition of *Manual del Cantinero* by John B. Escalante.

Queen's Cocktail

I f you want to become thoroughly confused about the origin of a drink named for a borough of New York City, read back issues of the *Brooklyn Daily Eagle*. During the 1930s, the *Eagle* covered the invention of—when not outright inventing—drinks named for Brooklyn and Queens, even though recipes already existed for both. The recipe below comes from Harry Craddock's 1930 *Savoy Cocktail Book*. Similar recipes appear in Albert Stevens Crockett's 1931 *Old Waldorf-Astoria Bar Book* and Patrick Gavin Duffy's 1934's *Official Mixer's Manual*. But I know what you're thinking: Is this one named for the borough of Queens, or was it made to honor a particular queen, owing to that apostrophe? Fear not: Both Craddock and Stevens call it the "Queen's Cocktail" because back in the day it was spelled "Borough of Queen's" or the "Queen's Borough." (The borough is named for Catherine of Braganza, wife of King Charles II and queen of England, Scotland, and Ireland.)

> 1 ounce Beefeater® London dry gin
> ½ ounce Dolin dry vermouth
> ½ ounce Dolin Rouge sweet vermouth
> ½ slice of crushed pineapple

Shake well with ice, and strain into a chilled cocktail glass.

NOTE

A quick comparison reveals that this is essentially a Bronx (page 140) made with pineapple in place of the orange.

Boothby Cocktail

William "Cocktail Billy" Boothby, San Francisco's greatest pre-Prohibition bartender, plied his trade as head bartender at the Palace Hotel. The San Francisco News Company published *Cocktail Boothby's American Bar-Tender* in 1891, but this recipe didn't appear in it until a posthumous edition in 1930. That year, the *San Francisco Chronicle* described the drink as "a delectable Manhattan, with a champagne float—a drink that never the gods of high Olympus quaffed." Let's not quibble with that account.

> ½ ounce Dolin Rouge sweet vermouth
> 2 dashes orange bitters
> 2 drops Angostura bitters
> 1 bar spoon Champagne or sparkling wine
> cherry for garnish

Stir well with ice, strain into a chilled cocktail glass, top with sparkling wine, and garnish with a cocktail cherry.

NOTE

In the early days of the Great War, Boothby created what may be the first vodka variation on the Manhattan—if not the first vodka cocktail. He had witnessed a heated argument between a German and a Frenchman and sought to make a drink to please all combatant nations. It contained "English gin, Russian vodka, German kümmel, Hungarian apricot brandy, Italian vermouth brandy manufactured in Ghent, Belgium, and a dash of French Amer Picon. The German and the Frenchman stopped their argument long enough to try the cocktail. They liked it and ordered another, and then a third, and then a fourth. Their argument became less and less heated," and the belligerents eventually departed arm in arm.

Boothby called it the Peace Cocktail, and clearly the State Department should hire more bartenders.

Remember the *Maine*

Toward the end of Cuba's three-year War of Independence against Spain, President William McKinley dispatched the USS *Maine* to Havana Harbor to oversee American concerns there. On February 15, 1898, the ship exploded under suspicious circumstances, killing three quarters of the crew. Incited by the yellow journalism of Hearst and Pulitzer newspapers, America declared war on the Spanish kingdom to jingoistic cries of "Remember the *Maine*, to hell with Spain!" The drink first appears in Charles Baker Jr.'s *The Gentleman's Companion: The Exotic Drinking Book* (1939), in which he recalls enjoying this drink during the Cuban Revolution of 1933: "each swallow was punctuated with bombs going off on the Prado, or the sound of 3" shells being fired at the Hotel Nacional, then haven for certain anti-revolutionary officers."

- 1½ ounces Sazerac rye whiskey
- ¾ ounce Dolin Rouge sweet vermouth
- 1–2 teaspoons Cherry Heering
- ½ teaspoon absinthe, Pernod®, or Herbsaint
- 1 dash Peychaud's bitters
- lime or lemon peel for garnish

Stir well ("in clock-wise fashion—this makes it sea-going, presumably!") with ice, strain into a chilled cocktail glass, and garnish with a lime or lemon peel.

NOTE

President McKinley is one of my distant cousins, as is Antoine Peychaud, so this drink is a family specialty.

Scofflaw

During Prohibition, a man named Delcevare King in Quincy, Massachusetts, staged a contest to come up with a word that best described the "'lawless drinker' of illegally made or illegally obtained liquor." He offered a $200 prize and recruited as fellow judges the Reverend E. Talmadge Root, secretary of the Massachusetts Federation of Churches; and A. J. Davis, regional superintendent of the Anti-Saloon League of America. The winning word had to begin with the letter *S*, as in *sting*, and include "a word that might be linked to the statement of President Harding, 'Lawless drinking is a menace to the republic itself.'" Ironically, "Both on the golf course and inside the White House, Harding thumbed his nose at Prohibition. At the Chevy Chase Club, Harding would pause every few holes for a shot of whiskey from a bottle stashed inside his golf bag." Two people submitted "scofflaw" as the winning entry, and each received a hundred clams. Less than two weeks after the winning word was announced, a bartender named "Jock" at Harry's New York Bar in Paris (where imbibing remained legal) created the Scoff-Law Cocktail, which Patrick Gavin Duffy immortalized in his *Official Mixer's Manual*.

> 1–2 ounces Wild Turkey 101 rye whiskey
> 1 ounce Carpano dry vermouth
> ½ ounce grenadine
> ½ ounce lemon juice
> 1 dash orange bitters
> cherry or lemon peel for garnish

Stir or shake well with ice, strain into a chilled cocktail glass, and garnish with a cherry or lemon peel.

NOTE

Duffy's recipe calls for equal parts rye and vermouth.

Marconi Wireless

Credited as the inventor of radio technology, Guglielmo Marconi pioneered the wireless long-distance transmission of radio signals. Naturally, such a watershed technological breakthrough should have a drink named for it; it's the American way! In *The Old Waldorf-Astoria Bar Book*, Albert Stevens Crockett wrote that the Marconi wireless "first 'materialized' at the Bar of the Old Waldorf when the ancestor of what is now called the 'radio' began to raise its ghostly voice." Crockett had a habit of exaggerating what was invented at the Waldorf, so he no doubt claimed that wireless itself was invented there.

2 ounces Laird's 100 proof apple brandy
1 ounce Martini sweet vermouth
2 dashes Fee Brothers orange bitters

Stir well with ice, and strain into a chilled cocktail glass.

NOTE
If you can't find Laird's 100 proof Straight Apple Brandy, you can substitute Laird's AppleJack.

Cocktail à la Louisiane

Stanley Clisby Arthur's *Famous New Orleans Drinks* also gives us this classic. My friend Chris McMillian—legendary New Orleans bartender and fellow cofounder of the Museum of the American Cocktail—and I include it in what we call the New Orleans Trinity: three timeless cocktails all invented within 100 yards of one another. The Sazerac (rye, absinthe, Peychaud's), the Vieux Carré (Cognac, rye, vermouth, Bénédictine, Angostura, Peychaud's—page 166), and the Louisiane all contain similar ingredients, and all came into being within steps of the corner of Iberville and Royal streets in the French Quarter.

    ¾ ounce Sazerac rye whiskey
    ¾ ounce Dolin Rouge sweet vermouth
    ¾ ounce Bénédictine
    3 dashes absinthe, Herbsaint, or Pernod
    3 dashes Peychaud's bitters
      cherry for garnish

Stir well with ice, strain into a chilled cocktail glass, garnish with a cherry, and *laissez les bons temps rouler*!

Vieux Carré

Walter Bergeron invented this classic at the Hotel Monteleone on Royal Street in the French Quarter of New Orleans. It first saw print in Stanley Clisby Arthur's *Famous New Orleans Drinks & How to Mix 'Em* (1937). In those days the Quarter—also called the Vieux Carré, French for "old quarter"—was home to French Creoles, Italians, and assorted folks from the Caribbean, making it a uniquely diverse American place. Its namesake drink features a French brandy and liqueur, Italian vermouth, American whiskey, and Caribbean bitters, so you're drinking New Orleans history.

1 ounce Pierre Ferrand 1840 Original Formula Cognac
   or other brandy
1 ounce Sazerac rye whiskey
1 ounce Martini sweet vermouth
2 dashes Angostura bitters
2 dashes Peychaud's bitters
1 teaspoon Bénédictine
   lemon peel for garnish

Fill a heavy-bottomed rocks glass with large ice cubes. Add the brandy, whiskey, vermouth, and bitters, and stir gently. Top with the Bénédictine, garnish with a lemon peel, and *à votre santé!*

NOTE
The Friends of the Library Association have designated the Monteleone—as well as the Algonquin (page 153)—an official literary landmark for hosting great writers such as Truman Capote, William Faulkner, Ernest Hemingway, Eudora Welty, Tennessee Williams, and others, including some incredibly average writers, such as myself.

Matador

This delicious tequila variation on the Manhattan comes not from Spain or Mexico but from the *Café Royal Cocktail Book*, written by British bartender William J. Tarling, a one-time president of the United Kingdom Bartenders Guild, and published in London in 1937 by the guild. In the 1920s and '30s, bullfighting was all the rage, its popularity no doubt encouraged by the publication of Ernest Hemingway's writings, notably his 1926 novel, *The Sun Also Rises*, and his 1932 bullfighting treatise, *Death in the Afternoon.*

¾ ounce Milagro Silver Tequila
¾ ounce Martini dry vermouth
¾ ounce Ferrand dry Curaçao
lemon peel

Shake well with ice, and strain into a chilled cocktail glass. Squeeze a lemon peel over top, and discard or use as a garnish; it's up to you.

NOTE
This and the next Tarling drink (page 170) come from Jared Brown and Anistatia Miller's excellent book *The Mixellany Guide to Vermouth & Other Apéritifs.*

Sombrero

Here's another tequila variation from the pages of the *Café Royal Cocktail Book*, as on page 169. Published by the United Kingdom Bartenders Guild, the book offered a wide range of drinks. More than a few contain relatively exotic spirits of the day: tequila and vodka. Indeed, Tarling debuted no fewer than 14 tequila drinks, including the Jalisco, Metexa, Mexican Eagle, Picador, Pinequila, Rio Grande, Señorita, Tequardo, and Tia Juano. Originally only 1,000 copies of this classic text were printed, but fortunately Mixellany has published a facsimile edition.

> 1½ ounces Milagro Silver Tequila
> ¾ ounce Dolin dry vermouth
> ¾ ounce Dolin Rouge sweet vermouth
> lemon peel

Shake well with ice, and strain into a chilled cocktail glass. Squeeze a lemon peel over top, and discard or use as garnish.

Fourth Regiment

Charles Baker Jr., author of the inimitable *Gentleman's Companion* (1939), explains that the drink came to his "amazed attention by one Commander Livesey, in command of one of His Majesty's dapper little sloops of war, out in Bombay, A.D. 1931." The earliest known reference to the drink comes from a "bar recipe book" called *Drinks: How to Mix and How to Serve*, published in 1889, reissued by a company in Portland, Oregon, and renamed *282 Mixed Drinks from the Private Records of a Bartender of the Olden Days*. The original book apparently was "found when tearing down the old buildings on Burnside Street, Portland, Oregon. It was the private property of a bartender and dated 1889." If you're wondering what to do with those celery bitters you have on hand, now you know.

> 1 ounce Riverboat Rye® whiskey
> 1 ounce Carpano Antica Formula sweet vermouth
> 1 dash celery bitters
> 1 dash orange bitters
> 1 dash Peychaud's bitters
> lime peel for garnish

Stir well with ice, and strain into a chilled cocktail glass. Garnish with "a twist of green lime peel squeezed so as to deposit oil upon the waters after the drink is poured."

Churchill

Legendary Savoy Hotel bartender Joe Gilmore, who left us for that great hotel bar in the sky in December 2015, created this drink to commemorate a visit by Winston Churchill—and we know how fond of a good drink Churchill was. "Always remember that I have taken more out of alcohol than alcohol has taken out of me" ranks among his most memorable quotes, as does this drink among Scotch cocktails. It seems only fitting that the son of the would-be inventor of the Manhattan (his mum) has a whisky drink named for him, but strange as it sounds, young Winston initially didn't take to whisky. As a young officer in the British Army, Churchill spent several years stationed in India. At first, he "disliked the flavour intensely," but after five days "with absolutely nothing to drink, apart from tea, except either tepid water or tepid water with lime-juice or tepid water with whisky," he "grasped the larger hope" and overcame his "repugnance to the taste of whisky." Travel and hardship have a way of broadening a man's horizons. Let's drink to that, shall we?

> 1½ ounces Monkey Shoulder Scotch whisky
> ½ ounce Dolin Rouge sweet vermouth
> ½ ounce Cointreau
> ½ ounce freshly squeezed lime juice

Stir well with ice, and strain into a chilled cocktail glass.

VERMOUT DOLIN
CHAMBÉRY
LA PLUS ANCIENNE
FABRIQUE DE
VERMOUT DE
FRANCE
FONDÉE EN 1821
MEMBRE DU JURY
EXPOSITIONS UNIVERSELLES
PARIS 1900
MARSEILLE 1922
INVENTEUR DU VERMOUT DE CHAMBÉRY
IMP. GOUGENHEIM FR. LYON

Marianne

You'll find this gem of a cocktail within the discussions of Manhattan variations in David Embury's 1948 classic *The Fine Art of Mixing Drinks*. (This drink and the next technically fall after World War II, but they fit with the drinks created and enjoyed before and during, so I've placed them here.) Without adornment, Embury informs us that the Marianne is a "medium Manhattan but with Byrrh substituted for the Italian vermouth." Byrrh is another apéritif bitter enjoying a resurgence as part of the craft cocktail movement. (It's also delicious on the rocks.) It falls within the category of quinquina—a fortified wine, like vermouth—but with the addition of quinine.

> 1½ ounces Traverse City Whiskey Co. American Cherry
>   Edition bourbon
> ¾ ounce Dolin dry vermouth
> ¾ ounce Byrrh Grand Quinquina
> 1–2 dashes Angostura bitters
>   cherry for garnish

Stir well with ice, strain into a chilled cocktail glass, and garnish with a cocktail cherry.

NOTE

The chosen whiskey for this recipe is a delicious bourbon that features 100 pounds of Traverse City cherries steeped within each barrel. If ever a spirit was made for a Manhattan, this is it.

Vesper

an Fleming invented this drink for the immortal James Bond and featured it in *Casino Royale* (1953), the very first Bond novel. The recipe in the novel calls for three parts Gordon's gin, one part vodka, and half a part of Kina Lillet shaken (of course), strained into a coupe, and garnished with a lemon peel. But since then, much ink has been spilled about this drink, which wouldn't taste the same if you made it the same way now. Gordon's isn't what it was in the 1950s, having lowered its proof; Kina Lillet also changed its formula; and so on. Fleming himself acknowledged that maybe it's not all that topping a drink, old boy. On April 5, 1958, *The Guardian* quoted him as saying, "I proceeded to invent a cocktail for Bond (which I sampled some months later and found unpalatable)." Nevertheless, the Vesper has become a classic variation on the Martini, and thereby a grandchild of the Manhattan. Here's how to make it the way Bond would like it.

2¼ ounces Tanqueray® London dry gin

¾ ounce vodka

⅓ ounce Lillet® Blanc or Cocchi Americano

lemon peel for garnish

Shake well with ice, strain into a chilled coupe, and garnish with a lemon peel.

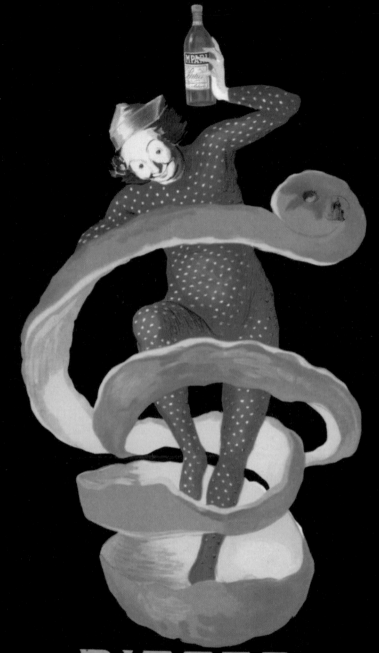

BITTER
CAMPARI

LA FAMIGLIA
AMERICANO

Thus far, the drinks we've seen build upon the spirits-vermouth-bitters platform. But a delightful set of drinks that shares that composition oddly enough descends from a spiritless drink. Originally called the Milano-Torino—named for the respective places of origin of Campari and Cinzano vermouth—the Americano married Campari, sweet vermouth, and charged water and earned its name from its popularity among Americans visiting Italy.

Most of us associate James Bond with his infamous martini, but the first drink ever to touch the lips of 007 was the Americano, which he ordered in a café in *Casino Royale*. Why the Americano? Just as there are bars where you're better off ordering beer, Bond held that "One cannot drink seriously in French cafés." Whenever in one, "Bond always had the same thing—an Americano—bitter Campari, Cinzano, a large slice of lemon peel and soda. For the soda he always specified Perrier, for in his opinion expensive soda water was the cheapest way to improve a poor drink."

From the Americano came the Negroni, then the Boulevardier and the Old Pal. These tremendous drinks will open the door to discovering the wonders of apéritif bitters, such as Aperol, Campari, Cocchi Americano, and many others, including a new offering from New Orleans, Peychaud's Aperitivo. *Salute!*

Americano

1 ounce Perrier
1 ounce Martini sweet vermouth
1 ounce Campari
orange or lemon peel for garnish

Fill a rocks glass with large ice cubes, add ingredients, and stir.
Garnish with an orange peel or, if you're feeling a bit 007, go with
lemon.

Negroni

1 ounce Hendrick's®, Ford's, or any good London Dry Gin
1 ounce Martini sweet vermouth
1 ounce Campari
orange peel for garnish

Fill a rocks glass with large ice cubes, add ingredients, and stir.
Garnish with an orange peel. (shown opposite)

Boulevardier

1 ounce Buffalo Trace bourbon whiskey
1 ounce Martini sweet vermouth
1 ounce Campari
orange peel for garnish

Fill a rocks glass with large ice cubes, add ingredients, and stir.
Garnish with an orange peel.

Old Pal

1 ounce WhistlePig® 100 proof rye whiskey
1 ounce Noilly Prat dry vermouth
1 ounce Campari
orange peel for garnish

Fill a rocks glass with large ice cubes, add ingredients, and stir.
Garnish with an orange peel.

21

CONTEMPORARY
VARIATIONS

Arecurring theme of the craft cocktail renaissance of the last 20-some years is the degree to which bartenders riff on the classics, offering their own unique variations on drinks such as the Old-Fashioned, Negroni, Sazerac, Daiquirí, and of course the Manhattan. Consider the enormous boom in whiskeys, from the rise of small-batch bourbons and ryes to the proliferation of microdistilleries. Then add the countless numbers of bitters on the market, the rediscovery of vermouth, and the increased availability and appreciation of apéritif bitters and amari from around the world, and it's a very good time to be sampling the many variations on the Manhattan's iconic foundation. To paraphrase Mao Tse-tung: There is great chaos in the cocktail heavens, and the situation is excellent. What follows are some of the more delicious variations that I've encountered.

Uptown Manhattan

n 1999, Marco Dionysos was bartending at Absinthe Brasserie & Bar—which specializes in French and northern Italian fare—in the Hayes Valley neighborhood of San Francisco. He entered a Maker's Mark® bourbon Manhattan competition, and, says Marco, "There was such interest in the competition that it was broken into five rounds of ten bartenders; one round a week for five weeks. The sixth week was the finals, pitting the winners of the five rounds against one another. I won my round, then took second place in the finals."

> 1¾ ounces Maker's Mark bourbon
> ½ ounce Amaro Nonino Quintessentia®
> 1 bar spoon Cherry Heering or other cherry brandy
> 1 dash orange bitters
> cherries and orange peel for garnish

Stir with ice, and strain into a chilled cocktail glass. Garnish with three brandied cherries and an orange twist.

The Morris

Jamie Boudreau—bartender at Canon, Seattle's whiskey and bitters emporium—created this cocktail in honor of Chris Morris, master distiller at Woodford Reserve, who kindly had shipped three bottles of Woodford Reserve® VIP Distiller's Select Bourbon Whiskey to Canon. Woodford sent this little care package as a way of thanking the tiny 40-seat bar for having sold more Woodford Reserve than any bar in the world. Boudreau now owns and runs Canon, which is known worldwide for its avant-garde cocktail program and for having one of the largest spirits collections in the world. A year after it opened, Canon won the Tales of the Cocktail® Spirited Award® for World's Best Drink List, and the establishment has received a James Beard Award nomination for Outstanding Bar Program three years running.

1½ ounces Woodford Reserve bourbon whiskey
1 ounce Lillet Blanc
½ ounce Amaro Nonino Quintessentia
1 dash Scrappy's Bitters® orange bitters
1 dash simple syrup
orange peel for garnish

Stir well with ice, strain into a chilled cocktail glass, and garnish with an orange peel.

The Maurice

n 2005, St. John Frizell quit his job as promotion copy director of *Bon Appétit* magazine to travel the world in the footsteps of Charles Baker Jr. When he returned to New York, he learned the art of bartending working with Audrey Saunders at Pegu Club (see page 195). Today he's an award-winning writer, bartender, and owner of the legendary café-bar Fort Defiance in the Red Hook neighborhood of Brooklyn. Frizell calls this his "best Manhattan variation." He based it on the Morris (page 186) and notes that "it's really a perfect(ish) Manhattan with the gentian liqueur doing the work of bitters."

> 1½ ounce Rittenhouse® rye
> ¾ ounce Cocchi Americano
> ½ ounce Carpano Antica Formula vermouth
> ¼ ounce Bittermens® Amère Sauvage
> lemon peel for garnish

Stir well with ice, strain into a chilled cocktail glass, and garnish with a lemon twist.

Black Manhattan

Todd Smith created this groundbreaking drink at Bourbon & Branch in the Tenderloin neighborhood of San Francisco, circa 2005. The drink initially was called the Harlem. His use of Averna®, a Sicilian amaro, in lieu of sweet vermouth, opened the door to further innovation. In 2014, Smith opened the celebrated ABV in San Francisco's Mission District along with Ryan Fitzgerald and Erik Reichborn-Kjennerud.

    2 ounces rye whiskey
    1 ounce Averna
    1 dash Angostura bitters
    1 dash Regans' Orange Bitters No. 6
    cherry for garnish

Stir well with ice, strain into a chilled cocktail glass, and garnish with a cocktail cherry.

Take Me Home, Country Roads

When Nick Crutchfield, now Diageo's master of whiskey, was working at Commonwealth Restaurant & Skybar in Charlottesville, Virginia, a customer asked for a Manhattan done Southern style. Cue up the John Denver song, and here's how:

> 1½ ounces George Dickel® No. 12 Tennessee Whisky
> ¾ ounce Dolin Rouge sweet vermouth
> ¾ ounce Art in the Age™ Root
> 1 dash Bad Dog Bar Craft Sarsaparilla Dry Bitters
> 1 dash Berg & Hauck's® Creole bitters or Peychaud's
> lemon peel for garnish

Stir well with ice, strain into a chilled cocktail glass, and garnish with lemon peel.

NOTE

Before root beer became nonalcoholic and what we now call root beer, it was called root tea and contained alcohol. (That, my friends, is actual irony.) The good folks at Art in the Age returned the drink to its origins, and Crutchfield used it to give his Manhattan some down-home Southern flavor.

Tale of Two Roberts

Several variations on the Scotch Manhattan (Rob Roy, page 137) take their name from Scotland's national poet—the Robert Burns, Robby Burns, and Bobby Burns—and incorporate additional ingredients such as absinthe, Bénédictine, and Drambuie®. Waldorf-Astoria bartender Frank Caiafa has created a splendid hybrid, which surely is called a Frank Burns, right? Not so, laddie. Of creating the Tale of Two Roberts, Frank says, "I recall a Repeal Day event where I simply combined the adorning components of the two classic Robert Burns cocktails (absinthe from the Old Waldorf Bar recipe and Bénédictine from the Savoy recipe). I recommend against adding any additional bitters as they break the link between the enhancing liqueurs and the robust vermouth provides more than enough heft on the herbal side."

> 2 ounces Spencerfield Spirit Sheep Dip® malt whisky or Johnnie Walker® Black Label blended Scotch whisky
> 1 ounce Cinzano Rosso sweet vermouth
> ¼ ounce Bénédictine liqueur
> 2 dashes Emile Pernot Vieux Pontarlier® absinthe
> lemon peel for garnish

Stir with ice for 30 seconds, strain into a chilled cocktail glass, and garnish with a lemon twist. For proper presentation, serve alongside three small shortbread cookies, "because who doesn't like freshly baked cookies?" Frank wisely notes.

Naphattan

This novel take on the Manhattan—created by H. Joseph Ehrmann of the award-winning Elixir in San Francisco's Mission District—replaces the vermouth with a simple homemade mixture of dry red wine and brown sugar. "I created this Shiraz–brown sugar syrup for a series of wine cocktails that I created and have found it useful in many recipes," says Ehrmann. "As usual, the simple ones are the best, and I found that it is a nice substitute for both the wine and sweetening effects of Italian vermouth. I also really like brown sugar with both bourbon and rye. Play around to find the whiskey you prefer, but I think you'll find this syrup a great addition to your bar."

> 2½ ounces Rittenhouse 100 proof rye
> ½ ounce Shiraz Brown Syrup (recipe below)

Fill a mixing glass with ice, add the ingredients, and stir for 20 seconds. Strain into a chilled cocktail glass, and garnish with a fresh cocktail cherry (see below).

FOR THE SYRUP

> 1 cup R. H. Phillips Night Harvest® Shiraz or other dry red wine
> 1 cup light brown sugar

In a saucepan, slowly heat the wine with the sugar, stirring until the sugar dissolves, then bring to a boil. Reduce the heat, and simmer 2 to 3 minutes. Allow the mixture to cool, then transfer to a squeeze bottle.

FOR THE CHERRY

Fill a mason jar or other sealable container with pitted, fresh cherries. (Leave the stems on for a nicer garnish.) Cover with maraschino liqueur, and allow to sit for several days.

Little Italy

n 1996, Audrey Saunders, now known as the Libation Goddess or Queen of Mixology, took a seminar led by Dale DeGroff, King of Cocktails. Three years later the royal duo opened Blackbird in Midtown East. In 2005, Saunders opened the now legendary Pegu Club in Manhattan's SoHo neighborhood, naming it after a colonial club for British officers and civil officials in Rangoon, Burma. Pegu Club helped galvanize the nascent craft cocktail renaissance. Like the Brooklyn-inspired drinks in the next chapter, the Little Italy is Audrey's homage to a New York neighborhood and uses Italian ingredients (but for the rye).

> 2 ounces Rittenhouse 100 proof rye
> ¾ ounce Martini sweet vermouth
> ½ ounce Cynar
> 2 Luxardo cherries for garnish

Stir well with ice, strain into a chilled cocktail glass, and garnish with the cherries.

Lion of Baltimore

n the War of 1812, the U.S. Navy was still a fledgling force,
so American privateers helped wreak havoc on British ships.
One of those American vessels was the *Lion of Baltimore*. In the
summer of 1814, the British, led by General Robert Ross, entered
Chesapeake Bay and attacked Washington, D.C. They burned
the White House and sacked the Capitol before taking aim at
Baltimore. They sent a naval squadron up the bay and found the
Lion hidden in Bodkin Creek. The British burned her to the
waterline but failed to capture Baltimore (prompting Francis Scott
Key to pen "The Star-Spangled Banner"). Maryland sharpshooters
later killed General Ross, whose body was preserved in a cask of
Jamaican rum and transported to Nova Scotia for burial. Today my
dad and I keep a sloop on Bodkin Creek, and I created this drink
in the summer of 2013 after sailing on the Chesapeake with him.
It began as a Jamaican Rum Manhattan, but I added lime juice
for brightness and orgeat to balance the sourness of the lime, and
Dale's amazing bitters add beautiful island flavors for fair winds and
following seas, hon.

 2 ounces Appleton Estate Reserve Blend Jamaican rum
 1 ounce Martini sweet vermouth
 ¾ ounce fresh lime juice
 ¼ ounce orgeat syrup
 2 dashes Dale DeGroff's Pimento Bitters®

Shake well with ice, and strain into a chilled cocktail glass.

Cargo Thief

Dead Rabbit Grocery & Grog in Manhattan's Financial District—named for one of New York's nineteenth-century Irish street gangs—has taken top honors for three years running at the Tales of the Cocktail Spirited Awards: World's Best New Cocktail Bar, World's Best Cocktail Menu, International Bartender of the Year, Best American Cocktail Bar, World's Best Drinks Selection, and World's Best Bar. They also have the largest selection of Irish whiskeys in New York. In other words, *have a drink there*. To formulate their peerless cocktail menu, cofounder Jack McGarry and bartender Jillian Vose recipe-tested countless cocktails, looking for unique twists on the classics. "Jack and I were going through some classic cocktails to start to build a database of recipes for consistency purposes," says Vose. "I would make my version of a classic, and he would make his. Then we would talk about what we liked and didn't like and morph the two ideas into a house spec we were both happy with. This drink is our house Manhattan . . . a very old spec spiced up with bitter Punt e Mes and our own Orinoco Bitters. The name is based on the life of John Morrissey, leader of the Dead Rabbit Gang in the mid-1800s. We named this drink after him to go along with his story that he was a cargo thief when he was in his teens to escape poverty." Enjoy this one in the Dead Rabbit's second floor cocktail bar, the drink as exquisite as the surroundings.

    1½ ounces Bulleit® rye
    1½ ounces house sweet vermouth
    ½ ounce Pierre Ferrand dry Curaçao
    4 dashes absinthe
    4 dashes Adam Elmegirab's Orinoco® bitters
    orange peel

Stir well with ice, and strain into a coupe or Nick & Nora glass. Twist an orange peel over the drink and discard.

NOTE

"Spec" is a bartending term for the proportions of ingredients in a recipe.

Preacher Man

Another Dead Rabbit original, this cocktail showcases how their bartenders like using two spirits as a base. Bartender Jesse Vida created it, and the name honors Lewis M. Pease, a Methodist minister and nineteenth-century reformer who played a role in bringing order to the Five Points. "This cocktail is a lot of my favorite things in a glass," Vida says. "I *love* mixing with crème de cacao and Amaro CioCiaro. They work very well together and compliment both the reposado tequila and the pot still Irish whiskey. Plus, who says you can't make a drink with an agave and whiskey base, eh? It's a variation on a perfect Manhattan that's rich in texture and has varying notes of chocolate with a long finish."

1 ounce Powers® John's Lane Irish whiskey
¾ ounce Siembra Azul® reposado tequila
½ ounce Carpano Antica Formula sweet vermouth
½ ounce dry vermouth
¼ ounce Amaro CioCiaro
¼ ounce crème de cacao
2 dashes absinthe
  orange peel for garnish

Stir well with ice, strain into a coupe or Nick & Nora glass, and garnish with an orange twist.

The Copperhead

J. P. Fetherston of Southern Efficiency in Washington, D.C., created this Manhattanesque take on the Diamondback, which is made with rye, applejack, and green Chartreuse. Southern Efficiency is one of three amazing and adjoining bars in D.C.'s Shaw neighborhood owned by my friend Derek Brown. (Mockingbird Hill and Eat the Rich are the other two, while the return of Derek's legendary speakeasy Columbia Room and the Passenger wait in the wings.) If you find yourself in the nation's capital, make time to visit Southern Efficiency and order this drink. If you don't, you can still make it at home with this recipe.

    1 ounce Rittenhouse 100 proof rye
    1 ounce Laird's Straight Apple Brandy
    ¾ ounce Cocchi Barolo Chinato
    1 bar spoon green Chartreuse
      cherry for garnish

Stir with ice, strain into a chilled coupe, and garnish with a brandied cherry.

Dale DeGroff's "Imperfect" Manhattan

I n 2014, Dale DeGroff—the King of Cocktails, cofounder of the Museum of the American Cocktail, and the first bartender ever named to the James Beard Foundation's Who's Who of Food and Beverage in America—was experimenting with various Manhattan recipes, wanting a vehicle to showcase his amazing new pimento bitters to the bartending community. As such, he didn't want any one flavor to dominate. He felt that, with a good, solid whiskey and a nice balance of either Dolin or Martini vermouth, he'd have a great backdrop against which his bitters could really shine—and they do!

> 2 ounces Knob Creek® rye whiskey
> ½ ounce Dolin Rouge sweet vermouth
> ¼ ounce Dolin dry vermouth
> 2 dashes Dale DeGroff's Pimento Bitters
> orange peel for garnish

Stir well with ice, and strain into a rocks glass containing one large ice cube. With a Y-shaped peeler or paring knife, cut a wide piece of orange peel. Twist it over the drink to express the oils, drop it in as a garnish, and serve.

22

THE SONS OF
BROOKLYN

The bulk of the recipes in this book descend directly from the Manhattan, but the following drinks are the Manhattan's grandchildren, so to speak. They all express variations on the theme of the Brooklyn Cocktail (page 145). All but one are named for Brooklyn neighborhoods and are beautiful examples of the versatility of the Manhattan framework as a basis for innovation.

As you'll notice, five of the seven recipes that follow come from bartenders who worked at one point or another at Milk & Honey. As such, I'd like to pause and pay my respects to the memory of Sasha Petraske, legendary founder of Milk & Honey, which opened in 1999 on New York's Lower East Side. Petraske's life ended too abruptly at the age of 42 in August 2015, but he leaves an indelible legacy: Milk & Honey arguably was the original modern-day speakeasy and forever changed how the world looks at craft cocktails. His mentorship and inspiration fostered innovation among his bartenders, as you'll see. Dale DeGroff offered these words on Petraske's impact on the profession: "Sasha was a decent and caring person, who was deeply ethical in his business practices. He made no fuss about it; he considered it normal human behavior. The 'all-business' crowd, informed only by profits and who practice ethical behavior on Sunday mornings exclusively, would call him naive. I wish there were more normal hearts in the world like Sasha."

Red Hook

J ust as the Manhattan launched a thousand drinks, so did Vincenzo Errico's Red Hook spark a firestorm of creativity. "That drink became a calling card, a secret handshake, back before there were cocktail bars on every corner," says Joaquín Simó (page 210). "If you walked into a bar and they not only knew how to make a Red Hook but had the ingredients to make it, you knew you were in a great spot." Errico created this cocktail at Milk & Honey New York in 2003. He has since returned to the country that gave us vermouth, and today he tends bar at L'Antiquario Napoli in Naples, Italy.

2 ounces rye whiskey
½ ounce Punt e Mes®
½ ounce maraschino liqueur
fresh cherry for garnish

Stir well with ice, strain into a chilled cocktail glass, and garnish with the cherry.

Greenpoint

Michael McIlroy invented this drink—another noteworthy adaptation of the Brooklyn to occur under the tutelage of owner Sasha Petraske—circa 2005. When Milk & Honey relocated to a larger location in 2013, McIlroy and fellow bartender Sam Ross opened Attaboy in the original Milk & Honey location, where it remains today.

    2 ounces rye whiskey
    ½ ounce yellow Chartreuse
    ½ ounce Punt e Mes
    1 dash Angostura bitters
    1 dash orange bitters
      lemon peel for garnish

Stir with ice, strain into a cocktail glass, and garnish with a lemon twist.

Bensonhurst

C had Solomon, cofounder of cocktail catering and consulting firm Cuffs & Buttons and co-creator and operator of Midnight Rambler in Dallas, named this Brooklyn variation after one of the borough's more tough-guy neighborhoods. "I was inspired to create the Bensonhurst," says Solomon, "particularly because of the distinct lack of original formula Amer Picon. In fall 2005, Pegu was the first account in New York to get Rittenhouse Bottled in Bond Rye Whiskey, and we were going ape-shit over it. There never was another candidate to anchor the cocktail. For dry vermouth, Noilly Prat was the original selection, but I switched to Dolin after Noilly Prat altered their dry vermouth formula. I was working at both Milk & Honey and Pegu Club; it was early 2006, and we were being egged on for new stirred and strong, bitter and boozy, aromatic-style drinks from our Pegu frontline regulars, Dave Wondrich, Sam Kinsey, Martin Doudoroff, Don Lee, and John Deragon. The cocktail made it on the Pegu Club's spring 2006 cocktail menu."

> 2 ounces Rittenhouse 100 proof rye
> 2 teaspoons Luxardo maraschino liqueur
> 1 teaspoon Cynar
> 1 ounce Dolin dry vermouth
> 2 drops mineral saline

Stir well with ice, and strain into a chilled cocktail or Nick & Nora glass.

NOTE

Mineral saline is a solution of 1 part kosher salt to 9 parts still mineral water, but just that tiny bit of salt gives the drink added dimension.

Carroll Gardens

Joaquín Simó created this drink at Death & Co. for the fall/winter menu of 2008. Now a partner in Alchemy Consulting and Pouring Ribbons in Manhattan's East Village, Simó was living in the Carroll Gardens neighborhood of Brooklyn when he invented the recipe. "Clearly, it's a nod to Enzo Errico's modern classic Red Hook Cocktail from 2004 at Milk & Honey. My contribution to this family of brown-and-stirred cousins nods to the Italian-American roots of Carroll Gardens. There are still tons of tiny little social clubs, Italian delis/butchers/bakers, and more Madonna-with-Child statues on the front-facing lawns of the brownstones on First through Fourth Place than you can shake a stick at. So every modifier is Italian in origin. A bittered sweet vermouth and a wonderfully complex bittersweet herbal liqueur add richness and balance each other, while a whisper of maraschino offers suggestions of stone fruit and marzipan."

2 ounces Rittenhouse 100 proof rye
½ ounce Punt e Mes
½ ounce Amaro Nardini
1 teaspoon Luxardo maraschino liqueur

Stir well with ice, and strain into a chilled cocktail glass.

Cobble Hill

S am Ross, who also invented the Penicillin Cocktail, created this when he too was bartending at the illustrious Milk & Honey in New York. An Aussie expat from Melbourne, Ross now lives and works in New York and owns the speakeasy-style Attaboy in Manhattan's Lower East Side.

> 3 cucumber slices, plus 1 extra for garnish
> 2 ounces rye whiskey
> ½ ounce Dolin dry vermouth
> ½ Amaro Montenegro®

Gently bruise three cucumber slices in a chilled mixing glass, then add the remaining ingredients and ice. Stir well, strain into a chilled coupe, and garnish with the last cucumber slice.

NOTE:
Don't confuse bruising with muddling. In Sam's words: "As this is a stirred drink, we don't want bits of the cucumber in the strained-off drink. Bruising or very lightly muddling releases the essence of the cucumber without muddying the visual presentation of the drink."

The Slope

This recipe hails from Julie Reiner, co-owner of Flatiron Lounge in Manhattan and Clover Club in Brooklyn and author of *The Craft Cocktail Party*. "This drink is our house Manhattan at Clover Club, and it has been a constant on the menu since we opened. It's also my house Manhattan at home; when friends come over for dinner, this is the cocktail I'll often push into their hands upon arrival."

 2½ ounces Bulleit, Wild Turkey, or other straight rye whiskey
 ¾ ounce Punt e Mes
 ¼ ounce Rothman & Winter Orchard Apricot liqueur
 2 dashes Angostura bitters
 2 Luxardo cherries for garnish

Stir well with ice, strain into a chilled Nick and Nora glass, and garnish with the cherries.

Bushwick

Phil Ward, co-owner of Mayahuel in New York City's East Village, created this drink in 2009. According to Ward, he "wasn't really trying to come up with a Brooklyn variation with this drink. Had been making it a lot with gin previously then just subbed out the gin for whiskey on the fly one time and really fell for it. Wasn't until I did it I realized it fit in the family."

  2 ounces Rittenhouse rye
  ¾ ounce Carpano Antica Formula vermouth
  ½ ounce Amaro Lucano®
  ¼ ounce maraschino liqueur
    lemon peel

Stir well with ice, and strain into a chilled cocktail glass. Twist a lemon peel over the drink and discard.

Big Chief

A bigail Gullo of Compère Lapin in New Orleans created this as her take on the Red Hook. A New York transplant, she notes that no additional bitters are needed because the bitters are in the Punt e Mes, making for a darker, deeper, richer Manhattan. The name comes from the Mardi Gras Indians tradition in the black community of New Orleans and a line from the classic Carnival song by Professor Longhair.

> 2 ounces Willett® Pot Still Reserve or Woodford Reserve bourbon
> ½ ounce Averna
> ½ ounce Punt e Mes
> orange for garnish

Stir well with ice, strain into a chilled cocktail glass, and garnish with a flamed orange disk.

NOTE

When making the drink with rye instead of bourbon, Gullo calls it the Longshoreman.

APPENDIX

Table of Select Pre-World War II Manhattan Recipes

Conversion Guide	1 gill = 4 ounces 1 jigger = 1½ ounces 1 pony = 1 ounce 1 wine glass = 3 ounces

Year	Author *Title* **Ratio of whiskey to vermouth**	Recipe Title
1884	**George Winter** *How to Mix Drinks: Bar Keepers' Handbook* **1:1**	**Manhattan Cocktail** *(Use large bar glass.)* Two or three dashes of Peruvian bitters; One to two dashes of gum syrup; One-half wine glass of whiskey; One-half wine glass of Vermouth; Fill glass three-quarters full of fine shaved ice, mix well with a spoon, strain in fancy cocktail glass and serve.
1884	**O.H. Byron** *The Modern Bartenders' Guide* **2:1**	**Manhattan Cocktail No. 1.** (A small wine-glass.) 1 pony French vermouth. 1 pony whisky. 3 or 4 dashes Angostura bitters. 3 dashes gum syrup.
1884	**O.H. Byron** *The Modern Bartenders' Guide* **1:1**	**Manhattan Cocktail No. 2.** 2 dashes Curacoa. 2 ' Angostura bitters. ½ wine-glass whisky. ½ ' Italian vermouth. Fine ice; stir well and strain into a cocktail glass.
1887	**Jerry Thomas** *The Bar-Tender's Guide or How to Mix Drinks* **2:1**	**Manhattan Cocktail.** *(Use small bar-glass.)* Take 2 dashes of Curaçoa or Maraschino. 1 pony of rye whiskey. 1 wine-glass of vermouth. 3 dashes of Boker's bitters. 2 small lumps of ice. Shake up well, and strain into a claret glass. Put a quarter of a slice of lemon in the glass and serve. If the customer prefers it very sweet use also two dashes of gum syrup.

1888	**Harry Johnson** *Bartenders' Guide* **1:1**	**Manhattan Cocktail** *(Use a large bar glass.)* Fill the glass up with ice; 1 or 2 dashes of gum syrup, very carefully; 1 or 2 dashes of bitters (orange bitters); 1 dash of curacao or absinthe, if required; ½ wine-glass of whiskey; ½ wine-glass of vermouth; Stir up well; strain into fancy cocktail glass; squeeze a piece of lemon peel on top, and serve; leave it for the customer to decide, whether to use absinthe or not. This drink is very popular at the present day. It is the bartender's duty to ask the customer, whether he desires his drink dry or sweet.
1891	**William T. Boothby** *Cocktail Boothby's American Bar-Tender* **1:1**	**Manhattan Cocktail** Into a small mixing-glass place one-quarter teaspoonful of sugar, two teaspoonfuls of water, three drops of Angostura, one-half jiggerful of whiskey, and one-half jiggerful of vermouth; stir, strain into a small bar glass, twist lemon peel and throw in and serve with ice water on the side.
1891	**Wehman Brothers** *Bartenders Guide: How to Mix Drinks* **1:1**	**Cocktail – Manhattan.** *(Use a large bar glass.)* Fill the glass with ice. Two or three dashes of gum syrup. One or two dashes of bitters. One dash of curacoa (or absinthe, if required) One-half wine-glass of whiskey One-half wine-glass of vermouth Stir up well, strain into a fancy cocktail glass, squeeze a piece of lemon peel on the top and serve.
1891– 1892	**William Schmidt** *The Flowing Bowl* **2:1**	**Manhattan Cocktail** Half a tumblerful of cracked ice 2 dashes of gum 2 dashes of bitters 1 dash of absinthe ⅔ drink of whiskey ⅓ drink of vino vermouth (A little maraschino may be added.) Stir this well, strain, and serve.
1893	**Manhattan Club** *New York Sun* **1:1**	?? The famous Manhattan cocktail was invented at the club. This consists of equal portions of vermouth and whisky, with a dash of orange bitters.
1895	**George Kappeler** *Modern American Drinks* **1:1**	**Manhattan Cocktail** Fill mixing-glass half-full fine ice, add two dashes gum-syrup, two Dashes Peyschaud (sic) or Angostura bitters, one half-jigger Italian vermouth, one-half Jigger whiskey. Mix, strain into cocktail-glass. Add a piece of lemon-peel or a cherry.

1895	**George Kappeler** *Modern American Drinks* **1:1**	**Manhattan Cocktail, Dry.** Prepare same as Manhattan Cocktail leaving out syrup and cherry.

Manhattan Cocktail, Extra Dry.
Mix same as Manhattan cocktail. Leave out syrup and cherry, and use French vermouth in place of Italian.

1895	**C. F. Lawlor** *The Mixicologist* **1:1**	Take 1 dash Schroeder's bitters

    1 half barspoonful syrup.
    ½ jigger vermouth.
    ½ jigger whiskey.
    2 dashes of maraschino
Stir well in glass previously filled with fine ice; strain in cool cocktail glass.
Author's note: This is likely sweet vermouth used here.

1898	*The Hotel/Motor Hotel Monthly, Volume 6* **1:1**	**Manhattan Cocktail**

    1 dash orange bitters
    1 dash Peychaud's bitters
    1 dash syrup
    ½ jigger whisky
    ½ jigger Italian Vermouth
    Piece of lemon peel
Strain into cocktail glass.

Manhattan Cocktail, Dry
Same as above, except omit the syrup.

1898	**Livermore & Knight** *Cocktails: How to Make Them* **1:1**	**Manhattan Cocktail** Fill mixing-glass half-full fine ice, add two dashes gum syrup, two Dashes Boker's bitters, one-half jigger Italian vermouth, one-half jigger whiskey. Mix, strain into cocktail-glass. Add a piece of lemon peel.

Manhattan Cocktai – Dry
Fill mixing-glass half-full fine ice, two dashes Boker's bitters, one-half jigger Italian vermouth, one-half jigger whiskey. Mix, strain into cocktail-glass. Add a piece of lemon peel.

Manhattan Cocktail – Extra Dry
Fill mixing-glass half-full fine ice, two dashes Boker's bitters, one-half jigger French vermouth, one-half jigger whiskey. Mix, strain into cocktail-glass. Add a piece of lemon peel.

1900	**James C. Maloney** *The 20th Century Guide for Mixing Fancy Drinks* **1:1**	**Manhattan Cocktail.** Fill mixing glass two-thirds full fine ice.

    1 piece lemon peel.
    1 teaspoonful syrup.
    1 or 2 dashes orange bitters.
    1 or 2 dashes Peychand's bitters.
    ½ wine glass Vermouth.
    ½ wine glass whisky (Hermitage).
Stir well and strain into cool cocktail glass and serve.

1900	James C. Maloney *The 20th Century Guide for Mixing Fancy Drinks* 1:1	**Manhattan Bell-Ringer** Fill mixing glass two-thirds full fine ice. ½ teaspoonful lemon juice. 1 teaspoonful syrup. 2 dashes orange bitters. 1 dash Peychaud's bitters ½ wine glass bourbon whiskey (Old Crow). ½ wine glass Vermouth While you are stirring the above mixture put one-half teaspoonful of abricotine into a cocktail glass, then rinse it so that he abricotine will be evenly coated all over inside of the cocktail glass, then strain and rub a piece of fresh cut lemon around the edge of the cocktail glass and serve.

The Col. Taylor "Manhattan Bell-Ringer."
Fill mixing glass two-thirds full fine ice.
2 teaspoonfuls of syrup.
½ teaspoonful lemon juice.
2 dashes orange bitters.
1 dash Peychaud's bitters
⅔ wine glass of Old Taylor bourbon.
⅓ wine glass of Vermouth (Italy).
Stir the above ingredients thoroughly and put one-half teaspoonful of abricotine into the cocktail glass, rinse it so that he abricotine will be evenly coated all over inside of cocktail glass, then strain and rub a piece of fresh cut lemon around the edge of the cocktail glass, then strain the mixture into it and serve.

1902	**Louis Fouquet** *Bariana* 1:1	**Manhattan Cocktail** Verre D Prendre le verre à mélange A, glace en petits morceaux, 2 traits d'angostura, 2 traits de noyaux, 3 traits de curaçao, finir avec rye whisky et vermouth de Turin en quantité égale, agiter, passer, verser, zeste de citron et servir.

1902	**Louis Fouquet** *Bariana* 1:1	**Manhattan Cocktail** Verre nº 5 Prendre le verre à mélange nº 1, mettre quelques morceaux de glace: 3 traits d'angostura bitter. Finir avec rye whisky et vermouth Turin, quantités égales, bien remuer, passer dans le verre nº 5. Servir avec un zeste de citron, une cerise ou une olive, au goût du consommatueur.

Manhattan Milk punch
Verre nº 10
Prendre le verre nº 10, le remplir à moitié de glace pilée:
2 cuillerées à café de sucre en poudre,
1 jaune d'oeuf frais,
1 verre à liqueur de madère,
1 verre à liqueur de rye whisky.
Remplir avec du lait, adapter un gobelet en argent, frapper fortement, saupoudrer la mousse de muscade, servir avec chalumeaux.

1902	**Louis Fouquet**
	Bariana
	1:1
		Manhattan Milk punch
		Punch Manhattan au lait chaud pour 10 personnes
		Dans un bol à punch en porcelaine:
		    250 grammes de sucre en poudre,
		    ½ litre d'eau chaude pour fondre le sucre.
		Faire chauffer ensemble:
		    ½ litre de rye whisky,
		    ½ litre de madère.
		Verser sur le sucre fondu, ajouter 2 litres de lait chaud,
		remuer, servir dans le verre n° 10.

1903	**Tim Daly**
	Daly's Bartenders'
	Encyclopedia
	1:1
		Manhattan Cocktail.
		Use a mixing glass.
		Half fill with fine ice.
		    1 dash of Angostura bitters.
		    ½ wine-glass of whiskey.
		    ½ wineglass of vermuth.
		Stir with spoon, strain into a cocktail glass, put in a cherry or olive, and serve.
		One that is a dear and lasting friend to the Bohemians, and probably called for more extensively than any other morning favorite.

1904	**Paul E. Lowe**
	Drinks as They Are
	Mixed
	1:1
		Use mixing glass. Ice, fine, fill glass.
		    Syrup, ½ barspoonful.
		    Angostura bitters, 1 dash.
		    Vermouth, ½ jigger.
		    Whiskey, ½ jigger.
		    Lemon peel, 1 piece twisted.
		Stir and strain into cool cocktail glass.

1905	**Christine** **Terhune Herrick,** **M. Harland** *Consolidated* *Library of Modern* *Cooking and* *Household Recipes* 2:1	**Manhattan Cocktail** Shake thoroughly the following: 2 dashes of curaçoa or maraschino, 1 pony of rye whiskey, 1 wineglassful of vermouth, 3 dashes Boker's bitters, and 2 small lumps of ice. Then strain into a claret glass. Add a slice of lemon, and, to make very sweet, two dashes of gum syrup.
1905	**The Gorham Co.** *Cocktails: How to* *Make Them* 1:1	**Manhattan Cocktail** Fill mixing-glass half-full fine ice, add two dashes gum syrup, two Dashes Boker's bitters, one-half jigger Italian vermouth, one-half jigger whiskey. Mix, strain into cocktail glass. Add a piece of lemon peel.

1906	**Louis**
	Muckensturm
	Louis' Mixed
	Drinks with Hints
	for the Care
	& Serving of Wines
	2:1
		Manhattan Cocktail
		    Take two dashes of orange bitters,
		    One dash of Angostura bitters,
		    One dash of Curacao,
		    One liqueur-glass of Italian Vermouth, and
		    Two liqueur-glasses of Rye whiskey.
		Fill the mixing-glass with ice; stir well and strain into a cocktail-glass.

1908	Jack Grohusko	Manhattan Cocktail
	Jack's Manual of	1 dash Boker's Bitters
	Recipes for Fancy	50% Italian Vermouth
	Mixed Drinks	50% rye whiskey
	and How to Serve	½ glass cracked ice.
	Them	Stir, strain and serve.
	1:1	

1912	Wehman Bros.	Cocktail – Manhattan.
	Bartenders' Guide	*(Use a large bar glass.)*
		Fill the glass with ice.
		Two or three dashes of gum syrup.
		One or two dashes of bitters.
		One dash of curacoa (or absinthe, if required)
		One-half wine-glass of whiskey
		One-half wine-glass of vermouth
		Stir up well, strain into a fancy cocktail glass, squeeze a
		piece of lemon peel on the top and serve.

1913	Harry Montague	Cocktail, Manhattan
	The Up-to-Date	Fill mixing glass with fine ice.
	Bartender's Guide	2 dashes syrup.
	1:1	1 dash Angostura bitters
		½ jigger vermouth.
		½ jigger whiskey.
		1 piece twisted lemon skin.
		Stir; strain into cocktail glass and serve.

1914	Jacques Straub	Manhattan Cocktail
	Drinks	1 dash Angostura bitters.
	2:1	⅓ jigger Italian vermouth.
		⅔ jigger bourbon. Stir.
		Manhattan, Jr., Cocktail
		Manhattan with orange peel. Shake well.

1914	L. & M.	Manhattan Cocktail
	Ottenheimer,	*Use large bar-glass.*
	Publishers	Fill up with shaved ice.
	New Bartender's	Two dashes of gum syrup.
	Guide	Three dashes of Angostura bitters.
	1:1	½ wine-glass of Vermouth.
		½ wine-glass of whiskey.
		Stir well; strain into cocktail-glass; twist a piece
		of lemon peel on top and serve.

1917	Hugo Ensslin	Manhattan Cocktail (Dry)
	Recipes for Mixed	⅔ Whiskey
	Drinks	⅓ Italian Vermouth
	2:1	2 dashes Angostura Bitters
		Stir well in mixing glass with cracked ice, strain and serve
		with an olive in glass and a lemon peel on top.

1917	**Hugo Ensslin**	**Manhattan cocktail (sweet)**
	Recipes for Mixed	Made same as Manhattan Cocktail (Dry) adding two dashes
	Drinks	gum syrup and serve with a cherry instead of an olive.
	2:1	

1922   **Robert Vermiere**   **Manhattan Cocktail.**
Cocktails: How to   Fill a bar glass half full of broken ice and add:
Mix Them   1 or 2 dashes of Angostura Bitters.
1:1   2 or 3 dashes of Gum Syrup or Curaçao.
                      ¼ gill of Rye Whiskey.
                      ¼ gill of Italian Vermouth.
                      1 dash of Absinthe if required.
Stir up well, strain into a cocktail-glass, add cherry, and squeeze lemon-peel on top. This is a very old, but still one of the best-known cocktails, named after the district in New York.

2:1   When required dry, use French Vermouth instead of Italian Vermouth. When desired medium, use:
¼ gill of Rye.
⅛ gill of French Vermouth
⅛ gill of Italian Vermouth.

1930   **Harry Craddock**   **Manhattan Cocktail (No. 1)**
The Savoy Cocktail   *Use small Bar glass.*
Book   2 dashes of Curaçao or Maraschino.
3:1   1 Pony Rye Whisky.
                      1 Wineglass Vermouth (Mixed).
                      3 Dashes Angostura Bitters.
                      2 Small Lumps of ice.
Shake up well, and strain into a claret glass. Put a quarter of a slice of lemon in the glass and serve. If preferred very sweet add two dashes gum syrup.

2:1   **Manhattan Cocktail (No. 2)**
⅔ Canadian Club Whisky.
⅓ Ballor Italian Vermouth.
Shake well, strain into cocktail glass, with cherry.

1:1   **Manhattan Cocktail (Sweet)**
½ Italian Vermouth.
½ Rye or Canadian Club Whisky.
Stir well and strain into cocktail glass.

Manhattan Cocktail (Dry)
¼ French Vermouth.
¼ Italian Vermouth.
½ Rye or Canadian Club Whisky.
Stir well and strain into cocktail glass.

1932	**James A. Wiley & Helene M. Griffith** *The Art of Mixing* **2:1**	**Manhattan Cocktail** With 1 dash of Angostura bitters put ⅔ Rye Whiskey and ⅓ Italian Vermouth. Ice well, shake well, pour well, drink— well, as few as you care to. Serve with cherry.
1934	**Patrick Gavin Duffy** *Official Mixer's Manual* **2:1**	**Manhattan Cocktail (Dry)** ⅔ Whiskey. ⅓ Italian Vermouth. 2 dashes Angostura Bitters Stir well with cracked ice, strain and serve with an Olive and a twist of Lemon Peel on top. Use glass number 2.
		Manhattan Cocktail (Sweet) Made same as Manhattan (dry) adding 2 dashes Gum Syrup and serve with a Cherry instead of an Olive. Use glass number 2.
1937	**Stanley Clisby Arthur** *Famous New Orleans Drinks & How to Mix 'Em*	**Manhattan Cocktail** 1 lump sugar 1 dash Peychaud bitters 1 dash Angostura bitters ½ jigger rye whiskey ½ jigger Italian vermouth 1 slice lemon peel Drop a lump of sugar in a bar glass, moisten with a very little water, dash on it the two Bitters, and crush with a barspoon. Add the rye whiskey (don't use Bourbon) and then the vermouth. Drop several lumps of ice into the glass and stir. After straining into the cocktail glass, twist a bit of lemon peel over the mixture to extract the atom of oil, drop in a maraschino cherry with a very little of the syrup.

NOTES

xiii   **blazed a trail for all others to follow.** Lucius Beebe, *The Stork Club Bar Book* (New Day Publishing, 2003), 19.

xiii   **the finest cocktail on the face of the Earth.** Gary Regan, *The Joy of Mixology* (New York: Clarkson Potter Publishers, 2003), 285.

2   **is ready to swallow any thing else.** *Balance and Columbian Repository* (Hudson, NY), May 13, 1806.

3   **wound its way to upper Market Street.** William Grimes, *Straight Up or on the Rocks: The Story of the American Cocktail* (New York: North Point Press, 2001), 79.

3   **to enjoy a social glass.** Edward S. Stokes, *The Hoffman House: Its Attractions* (New York: Campbell Book Presses, 1885), 19–20.

4   **until at last it does become public property.** "With the Clubmen" column, written by "Bobbie," *New York Times,* June 29, 1902.

4   **William invents a new drink every day.** *Philadelphia Inquirer,* December 8, 1893.

4   **the grand cocktail!** *New York Times,* May 6, 1904.

5   **ensuring its ensuing popularity.** Jared Brown & Anistatia Miller, *The Mixellany Guide to Vermouth & Other Apéritifs* (Cheltenham: Mixellany Limited, 2011), Kindle version, 590 of 2693.

5   **when Claudius Prat joined the firm.** Paul Clarke, "The Truth About Vermouth," *San Francisco Chronicle,* August 15, 2008.

5   **Rhône-Alpes region of southeastern France.** Brown & Miller, *The Mixellany Guide,* Kindle version, 670 of 2693.

10   **exported 612,000 liters of it to America.** Brown & Miller, *The Mixellany Guide,* Kindle version, 128–131.

12   **gentlemen of nice perceptions and delicate tastes.** *New York Herald,* February 5, 1893.

12   **known to enjoy vermouth cocktails.** *Rock Island Argus,* January 2, 1883.

12   **they don't break you up.** *Wisconsin State Journal,* March 6, 1885.

13   **jumped from 427,644 to 656,424 during that same period.** Thirty-Sixth Annual Report of the Corporation of the Chamber of Commerce of the State of New York for the Year 1893–94 (New York: Press of the Chamber of Commerce, 1894), 47.

13   **a glass of vermouth and bitters.** *New York Sun,* May 30, 1890.

14   **which is also a vermouth cocktail.** *Kansas City Times,* January 26, 1896. Syndicated story originally in the *New York Sun.*

15   **plain whiskey cocktails and Manhattans.** *St. Louis Republic,* May 24, 1896.

15   **the initial feature that led to their popularity.** Livermore & Knight, *Cocktails: How to Make Them* (Providence, RI: Livermore & Knight Co., 1898), 9.

15   **most famous of the varieties on the market.** *New York Times,* June 15, 1899.

15   **whose life and professional pride is tied with it.** Otto Jacoby, Berkeley Yeast Laboratory, from a 1948 article in *Wines and Vines,* quoted in Adam Ford, *Vermouth* (Woodstock, VT: Countryman Press, 2015), 108.

16   **with, well, just about everything.** David Wondrich, *Imbibe! Updated and Revised Edition: From Absinthe Cocktail to Whiskey Smash, a Salute in Stories and Drinks to "Professor" Jerry Thomas, Pioneer of the American Bar* (New York: Perigee Books, 2015), 250.

16   **like *Listeria* in warm egg salad.** Wondrich, *Imbibe!,* 268.

16   **at that world famous resort.** *Boston Herald,* November 25, 1904.

16   **outside over the roofs of the town.** Ernest Hemingway, *A Farewell to Arms* (New York: Charles Scribner's Sons, 1929), 85.

17   **with Angostura bitters.** Ernest Hemingway, "There She Breaches! Or, Moby Dick off the Morro," *Esquire,* April, 1936. Reprinted in *By-Line: Ernest Hemingway,* ed. William White (New York: Charles Scribners Sons, 1967).

17 **in the shadow by Fouquet's bar.** F. Scott Fitzgerald, *Tender Is the Night* (New York: Charles Scribner's Sons, 1934, 1982), 95.

17 **a demijohn of angostura bitters.** Shake. F. Scott Fitzgerald, *On Booze* (New York: New Directions Publishing Corp., 2009), 7–8.

18 **to U.S. Senator Everett Dirksen.** Mark Will-Weber, *Mint Juleps with Teddy Roosevelt: The Complete History of Presidential Drinking* (Washington, DC: Regnery History, 2014), 295–96.

19 **by prefixing "Manhattan."** *Amsterdam Daily Recorder,* April 17, 1917.

19 **briefly mentioned the story in 1911.** Cocktail sleuths beware: this story is often mistakenly cited as being from 1877, due to Google Books inexplicably appending a batch of *1911 LaFollette's Magazines* into the middle of an 1877 *Catalogue of the Brooklyn Library.* I hate to break it to you, but sometimes things you find on the Web just aren't correct.

19 **its name banned in polite society.** *LaFollette's Weekly Magazine* 3, no. 45 (November 11, 1911): 10.

20 **but the Manhattan did.** *New Orleans Times-Picayune,* September 22, 1954.

20 **from his early days as a reporter.** *Frederick (MD) Post,* January 19, 1982.

20 **we amateurs discovered them years ago.** Email exchange with Professor John Baer, May 6, 2015.

20 **it was complete hogwash.** *New York Evening Mail,* December 28, 1917.

20 **while advocating his public health policies.** *Boston Herald,* September 17, 1952.

20 **about the Kennedy White House.** *Baton Rouge State-Times Advocate,* February 10, 1962.

21 **Unheard of Presidents' Day Sale.** *Wall Street Journal,* February 18, 2010.

22 **by columnist Philip Hale.** *Boston Herald,* March 26, 1911.

22 **large shareholder in the Brewing Association.** *New Orleans Daily Picayune,* May 20, 1893.

22 **largest billiard saloon on the continent.** *New Orleans Daily Picayune,* December 24, 1875.

22 **prepared in the highest style of art.** *New Orleans Daily Picayune,* December 24, 1875

24 **which became a leading resort.** *New Orleans Daily Picayune,* June 25, 1893.

24 **Walker did travel to New York.** *New Orleans Daily Picayune,* October 22, 1884.

26 **southwest corner with 15th Street.** *Omaha World Herald,* January 14, 1894.

26 **most social years of the Manhattan.** *New York Sun,* October 10, 1915.

26 **a princely sum in those days.** *Cleveland Plain Dealer,* May 21 1893.

26 **members could dine al fresco.** New York Sun, October 10, 1915.

28 **excellent cuisine, wine, and cigars.** *New York Herald,* April 2, 1893.

28 **with a dark brown taste in their mouths.** *New York Herald,* December 18, 1887.

28 **the Manhattan Club has invented another.** *Buffalo Courier,* August 28, 1873. Originally run by the *New York Sun.*

29 **the Manhattan Club's rooms in New York.** Wondrich, *Imbibe!,* 254.

29 **always drink oyster and Manhattan cocktails.** *New York Herald,* April 2 1893.

30 **at any other place in the country.** Don't worry, I'll get into a few of these "famous drinks" later on.

30 **with a dash of orange bitters.** *Cleveland Plain Dealer,* May 21, 1893, reprinting a New York Sun story.

31 **and hence their freight.** *Life,* volume 8, July–December 1886.

31 **An outrage.** *New York Herald,* November 22, 1892.

31 **was in bed and asleep.** *New York Herald,* November 22, 1892.

32 **Portland newspapers in 1888 and 1889.** *The Oregonian,* March 4, 1889.

32 **giving to the world the Manhattan Cocktail.** *Milwaukee Sentinel,* August 28, 1915, reprinting a story originally run in the *Providence Journal.*

34 **the event Mr. Gibbs speaks of.** *Catering Industry Employee*, March 19, 1945.

34 **didn't occupy that house until around 1890.** *New-York Tribune Illustrated Supplement*, January 20, 1901.

34 **his book had first appeared in 1860.** William Grimes, *Straight Up or on the Rocks* (New York: North Point Press, 2001), 62.

36 **prevailed among the vast throng.** *Albany Argus*, December 31, 1874.

39 **"some anonymous genius" at the club.** Wondrich, *Imbibe!*, 255.

39 **"famous as an after dinner speaker."** *New York Sun*, October 10, 1915.

41 **'but that's even worse.'** James Villas, *Villas at Table: A Passion for Food and Drink* (New York: Harper & Row, 1988), 74.

41 **dates to June 7, 1883.** *Cleveland Daily Leader*, June 1883.

42 **most famous mixed drink in the world in its time.** William F. Mullhall, "The Golden Age of Booze," a chapter from *Valentine's Manual of Old New York* (New York: Valentine's Manual, Inc., 1922), 134.

43 **that bar patronized by connoisseurs.** *New York Evening World*, October 11, 1887.

43 **fabricator in chief of the soothsome 'sour.'** *New York Herald*, December 17, 1886.

43 **until the next morning.** *New York Herald*, February 18, 1887.

44 **hats by Charles Webb.** *Trow's New York City Directory*, May 1, 1872.

45 **drink of the substantial man.** William Grimes, *Straight Up or on the Rocks* (New York: North Point Press, 2001), 74–75.

45 **anything that can be manufactured.** *Boston Herald*, December 9, 1883.

45 **a juicy and delicious compound.** *New Orleans Times-Democrat*, as reprinted in the *Omaha Daily Bee*, July 23, 1885.

45 **Make a Man Feel Like a King.** *St. Paul Daily Globe*, September 19, 1886.

45 **the secret of making a Manhattan.** *Atlanta Constitution*, March 23, 1890

47 **serve it out regularly.** *Chicago Tribune*, November 25, 1883.

47 **the most drunk of all mixed drinks.** *New York Herald*, July 5, 1891.

50 **William Schmidt in 1891.** William Schmidt, *The Flowing Bowl* (New York: Charles L. Webster, 1891).

50 **Louis Muckensturm in 1906.** Louis Muckensturm, *Louis' Mixed Drinks with Hints for the Care & Serving of Wines* (Boston: Caldwell, 1906), 35.

50 **Jacques Straub in 1914.** Jacques Straub, *Drinks* (Chicago: Hotel Monthly Press, 1914), 31.

50 **Hugo Ensslin in 1916.** Hugo Ensslin, *Recipes for Mixed Drinks* (n.p.: n.p., 1916).

50 **Patrick Gavin Duffy in 1934.** Patrick Gavin Duffy, *Official Mixer's Manual* (New York: R. Long and R. R. Smith, 1934), 119.

50 **at least one-quarter of the drink.** Gary Regan, *The Joy of Mixology* (New York: Clarkson Potter Publishers, 2003), 286.

52 **extended to the Pacific Coast.** "Cherry in the Cocktail," *Mixer and Server* 20, no. 5 (May 1911): 64.

52 **with one movement of his hand.** *Brooklyn Daily Eagle*, July 3, 1900.

52 **as surely as a bad check.** *New York Tribune Illustrated*, December 25, 1904.

53 **the gentle young thing.** *New York Tribune Illustrated*, December 25, 1904. See also the *Columbus Daily Enquirer*, March 4, 1899. Essentially the same story appears in both papers, with only minor variations in the telling.

54 **an onion in the house.** *Our Paper* (MA), April 16, 1916, p. 168.

56 **Huh! ain't no such thing.** *New York Sun*, December 15, 1889.

56 **the dusty way to failure.** *New Haven Register*, October 27, 1891.

57 **after takin' a dose.** *Brooklyn Daily Eagle*, November 17, 1901.

57 **that can be manufactured.** *Boston Herald*, December 9, 1883.

57 **ginger in the cocktail.** *New York Sun*, April 22, 1913.

58 **he thought he was poisoned.** *Brooklyn Daily Eagle*, March 15, 1906.

58   I haven't an egg in the house. *Goodwin's Weekly* (Salt Lake City, UT), September 16, 1911, p. 15.

59   period of high political hopes. *Richmond (VA) Times-Dispatch*, September 21, 1911.

61   as anything but a joke. *Cleveland Plain Dealer*, September 28, 1907.

61   the V.-P. is innocent! *Montgomery Advertiser*, July 10, 1907.

64   to eat a hot dog. *Spokane Spokesman Review*, April 2, 1951.

64   semi-barbarians of the Old World. *Chicago Tribune*, May 31, 1885.

65   the insidious "gin fizz." *Columbus Daily Eagle*, August 25, 1893.

65   versatile toddy slingers. *Washington Star*, November 6, 1886.

65   ten to one on the cocktail. As reprinted in the *Kansas City Times*, July 26, 1887.

65   stirred to the uttermost. *St. Paul Daily Globe*, July 28, 1887.

65   "Yes, sir." Stephen Crane, *Denver Rocky Mountain News*, May 19, 1895.

65   the seductive Manhattan cocktail. *Kalamazoo Gazette*, November 25, 1897.

66   anything you can get in New York. *Brooklyn Life*, October 28, 1899.

66   the Bronx and Clover Club. *Klamath Falls (OR) Evening Herald*, March 20, 1920.

67   tasted outside of America. *Kalamazoo Gazette*, April 15, 1900.

68   I'll drink mine. *The Day Book* (Chicago), August 30, 1913.

68   and coloring matter. *Miami Herald*, March 28, 1915.

69   Here's how. *Aberdeen (SD) Daily News*, October 5, 1918.

70   a small square of white bread. *Boston Herald*, December 16, 1933.

71   and the Daiquirí. "There are hundreds of cocktails which have jumped into prominence since Repeal, but there is none with has begun even to threaten the tremendous popularity of the 'Big Four'—the Martini, the Manhattan, the Old-Fashioned and the Side Car." Okay, I might have to quibble with the *Sacramento Bee* of December 12, 1940, on the Sidecar, a lovely drink, but I think the Daiquirí gets the nod.

71   in his top five. *Brooklyn Daily Eagle*, March 17, 1935.

71   the Jack Rose and Sidecar. David Embury, *The Fine Art of Mixing Drinks* (New York: Doubleday & Company, 1948), 121–122.

76   I'd stick to beer. *San Diego Union*, September 8, 1910.

77   How's about it . . . *Brooklyn Daily Eagle*, January 28, 1934.

77   Falling Downnnnnnn. *Brooklyn Daily Eagle*, January 31, 1934.

78   your nearest neighbor. *Brooklyn Daily Eagle*, February 4, 1934.

78   the usual icing and shaking. *Brooklyn Daily Eagle*, February 8, 1934.

78   strain into a cocktail glass. *Brooklyn Daily Eagle*, February 10, 1934.

79   and do things about it. *Brooklyn Daily Eagle*, February 10, 1934.

79   oh suh-well! *Brooklyn Daily Eagle*, December 20, 1934.

79   it shakes you up. *Brooklyn Daily Eagle*, December 6, 1935.

79   the new version. *Brooklyn Daily Eagle*, January 15, 1937.

80   a teaspoon of powdered sugar. *Brooklyn Daily Eagle*, February 19, 1937.

80   and be shaken. *Brooklyn Daily Eagle*, February 26, 1937.

80   a twist of orange peel. *Brooklyn Daily Eagle*, February 26, 1937.

80   the St. George as its birthplace. Salvatore Calabrese, *Classic Cocktails* (New York: Sterling Epicure, 2015), 108.

81   a new fashioned old-fashioned. *Trenton Evening Times*, December 17, 1945.

82   ". . . readily available," he said. Robert Simonson, "Cocktails for the History Books, Not the Bar," *New York Times*, May 14, 2012.

82   They were right. Wondrich, *Imbibe!*, 283.

83   with orange bitters. *New York Herald,*
      September 18, 1892.

83   another of the same kind. *Kalamazoo
      Gazette,* April 17, 1901.

86   as she gulped it off. *Brooklyn Daily Eagle,*
      July 25, 1902.

87   drank at the table. *Albuquerque Journal,*
      June 19, 1909.

87   bristle with cocktails. *New York Times,*
      June 23, 1909.

87   introduced into evidence. *Albuquerque
      Journal,* June 23, 1909.

90   I've never made them before. *Brooklyn
      Daily Eagle,* December 30, 1942.

93   for several days afterward. *St. Paul Daily
      Globe,* December 2, 1888.

94   to drink their cocktails. *New York Times,*
      May 19, 1893.

95   wisely crept away. *Charleston (SC) News
      and Courier,* December 4, 1895. Originally
      in the *New York Herald,* November 29,
      1895.

95   stimulate appetite and digestion. George
      C. Johnston, *Maryland Medical Journal* 45,
      no. 2 (February 1902): 62.

95   same advice the same year. *Journal of the
      American Medical Association* 39 (December
      6, 1902): 1443.

95   known to be intoxicating. *Michigan Law
      Review* 7 (1908–1909): 3369.

96   lower the guest to the ambulance. *San
      Francisco Chronicle,* October 21, 1911.

96   limited it to one. *Baton Rouge State Times
      Advocate,* July 18, 1932.

96   burglars liked Manhattan cocktails.
      Brooklyn Daily Eagle, November 20, 1938.

98   on a trip to Washington. *Augusta
      Chronicle,* December 1, 1963.

98   she had an inner-ear imbalance. Will-
      Weber, *Mint Juleps,* 272.

98   sure to delight her audience. *Miami News,*
      December 17, 1928.

98   a moving, thrilling melodrama. *Reading
      (PA) News,* November 27, 1928.

100   the night-lit street. Dashiell Hammett,
      The Maltese Falcon (New York: Alfred A.
      Knopf, Inc., 1930), 52.

100   booze on our belts. Jack Kerouac, *Big Sur*
      (New York: Penguin Group, 1962).

102   coffee machines in the office. *Lexington
      Herald-Leader,* July 9, 1961.

102   the manufacture of his cocktail? *Trenton
      Evening Times,* April 16, 1963.

103   a retired bartender. Embury, *The Fine Art,*
      7.

103   we may see the unicorn. Bernard DeVoto,
      The Hour: A Cocktail Manifesto (Portland,
      OR: Tin House Books, 2010), 68.

105   a better place in which to live. Embury,
      The Fine Art, 21.

105   when it comes to the Martini, phooey!
      Embury, *The Fine Art,* 121.

105   than any other kind. Embury, *The Fine
      Art,* 121–122.

106   vermouth into your martinis. Ford,
      Vermouth, 111.

106   a whole canteen on vermouth? A. E.
      Hotchner, *Papa Hemingway* (New York:
      Random House, 1966), 107.

108   beverage behind bars today. Brown &
      Miller, *The Mixellany Guide,* 10.

108   while shaking the drink. Grimes, *Straight
      Up or On the Rocks,* 12.

109   quickly became an institution. Grimes,
      Straight Up or On the Rocks, 88.

109   smashed into a telephone pole. Ford,
      Vermouth, 107, quoting B. B. Turner, "The
      Importance of Vermouth," *Wines and Vines*
      22, no. 3 (1941).

109   martinis and manhattans. *Register Star*
      (Rockford, IL), May 1981.

109   Do you drink Manhattans? *Dallas
      Morning News,* November 9, 1983.

109   Margery Eagan asked in 1987. *Boston
      Herald,* October 18, 1987.

109   romantic or chic. Jay McInerney, *The
      Juice: Vinous Veritas* (London: Bloomsbury
      Publishing, 2012), 3.

110   it "never overpowers." Ford, *Vermouth,* 114.

110 **for the next thirty years.** Ford, *Vermouth*, 116.

110 **its second golden age.** Grimes, *Straight Up or on the Rocks*, 122, 126.

111 **their European counterparts.** Ford, *Vermouth* , 141.

117 **that led to their popularity.** Livermore & Knight, *Cocktails*, 9.

121 **any other place in the country.** *Cleveland Plain Dealer*, May 21, 1893. This article originally ran in the *New York Sun*.

123 **the best interests of the Club.** Henry Watterston, *The History of the Manhattan Club of New York- Fiftieth Anniversary* (New York: Manhattan Club, 1916), 30–31.

130 **evolved into the Dry Martini.** Gary Regan and Mardee Haidin Regan, *The Martini Companion: A Conoisseur's Guide* (Philadelphia: Running Press, 1997), 29–30.

135 **after 1880.** Wondrich, *Imbibe!*, 23, 29.

137 **almost anything.** Kingsley Amis, *Everyday Drinking: The Distilled Kingsley Amis* (New York: Bloomsbury USA, 2008), 170

138 **music with swing to it.** *Evansville (IN) Courier*, June 17, 1897.

138 **to the officer in charge.** *Washington Evening Star*, May 31, 1897.

138 **who overturned the verdict.** Eric Felten, "Making Bitter Fernet-Branca Much Easier to Swallow," *Wall Street Journal*, January 3, 2009, available online at http://www.wsj. com/articles/SB123092858411149807.

139 **sued the committee for $50,000!** *The Enterprise* (Helena, MT), June 23, 1910.

140 **the bruised spots of his spirit.** F. Scott Fitzgerald, *This Side of Paradise* (New York: Charles Scribner's Sons, 1920), 199–200.

140 **be careful of this one, folks!** Eric Felten, "A Toast to April 15," *Wall Street Journal*, April 15, 2006, online at http://online.wsj. com/articles/SB114504694150826369.

154 **without tasting it.** Dale DeGroff, *The Craft of the Cocktail* (New York: Clarkson Potter, 2002), 83.

157 **in Santiago de Cuba.** Jeff Berry, *Beachbum Berry's Potions of the Caribbean* (New York: Cocktail Kingdom, 2014), 111.

157 **now known as El Floridita.** Wondrich, *Imbibe!*, 289–292.

160 **the gods of high Olympus quaffed.** William T. Boothby, *Cocktail Boothby's American Bar-tender: The New Anchor Distilling Edition* (San Francisco: Anchor Distilling, 2009), foreword (no page numbers).

160 **called it the Peace Cocktail.** Boothby, *Cocktail Boothby's American Bar-tender*, foreword (no page numbers).

161 **makes it sea-going, presumably!** Charles Baker Jr., *The Gentleman's Companion: The Exotic Drinking Book* (New York: Crown Publishers, 1939, 1946), 116–117.

163 **illegally obtained liquor.** *Boston Herald*, January 16, 1924.

163 **a menace to the republic itself.** *Boston Herald*, January 16, 1924.

163 **a bottle stashed inside his golf bag.** Don Van Natta Jr., *First Off the Tee: Presidential Hackers, Duffers, and Cheaters from Taft to Bush* (New York: PublicAffairs, 2003), 263.

163 **created the Scoff-Law Cocktail.** Gary Regan, *The Joy of Mixology* (New York: Clarkson Potter, 2003), 332. See also http://chanticleersociety.org/cocktailtime/ Scofflaw.html.

163 **immortalized in his *Official Mixer's Manual*.** Patrick Gavin Duffy, *The Official Mixer's Manual* (New York: Blue Ribbon Books, 1934, 1940), 125 in 1940 edition.

171 **after the drink is poured.** Baker, *The Gentleman's Companion*, 36.

172 **repugnance to the taste of whisky.** Winston Churchill, *My Early Life: 1874–1904* (New York: Charles Scribner's Sons, 1930), 126.

176 **and found unpalatable.** Ian Fleming, "The Exclusive Bond, Mr. Fleming on His Hero," *Manchester Guardian*, April 5, 1958.

179 **to improve a poor drink.** Ian Fleming, "From a View to a Kill," *For Your Eyes Only*, (New York: The Viking Press, 1959), 9-10.

ACKNOWLEDGMENTS

In order of gratitude, I have to begin with my literary agent, Adam Chromy of Movable Type Management. Unlike my first book, this one wasn't my idea: Adam brought it to me and worked to make the deal with my publisher. Which brings us to the amazing team at Sterling Publishing, notably my great editor and good friend James Jayo, photo editor Linda Liang for her stellar image research, interior designer Christine Heun for masterfully translating the essence of the story into visual form, cover designer Elizabeth Lindy for the book's beautiful exterior, production editor Scott Amerman for keeping the book in line and on track, and the rest of the team. Thanks also to Ravi DeRossi, who kindly let us shoot in Death & Co; Alla Lapushchik, bartender and co-owner of Post Office Whiskey Bar and OTB, who deftly made the drinks that appear in the recipe shots; and photographer Max Kelly for his keen eye and expertise.

I couldn't have written this without the assistance of the following friends and colleagues. I'll start with David Wondrich, who was ridiculously generous with his knowledge, resources, and time. (Let's face it: Dave could've written this book—and probably better.) Thanks also go to Greg Boehm (Cocktail Kingdom) and Ethan Kahn (Mud Puddle Books) for their help with vintage cocktail books. Thanks also to Dale DeGroff, Liz Williams, Robert Simonson, Chris Hannah, Paul Clarke, Martin Doudoroff, Professor John Baer, Leah Painter Roberts, Robert Hess, Gary "Gaz" Regan, Adam Elmegirab, Anistatia Miller, Jared Brown, Adam Ford, Jason Horn, Derek Brown, Lynette Marrero, Amanda France, Francine Cohen, Noah Rothbaum, and Chris and Laura McMillan.

Let's not forget the bartenders who contributed their tremendous drinks: Todd Smith, Jamie Boudreau, St. John Frizell, Marco Dionysos, Nick Crutchfield, Frank Caiafa, H. Joseph Ehrmann, Audrey Saunders, Jack McGarry, Jillian Vose, Jesse Vida, J. P. Fetherston, Dale DeGroff, Vincenzo Errico, Michael McIlroy, Chad Solomon, Joaquin Simó, Sam Ross, Julie Reiner, Phil Ward, and Abigail Gullo. Special thanks go to the immortal Sasha Petraske.

I also must thank Lisa Laird Dunn, Charlotte Voisey, Han Shan, Jennifer Corrao, Audrey Fort, Eric Seed, Michael Chernoff, Jake Parrott, Caitlin Crisan, Stefanie Smith, Mark Brown, Kevin Richards, Meredith Moody, Stephanie

Schmidt, Laura Baddish, Abby Vinyard, Jenn Fruzetti, Giuseppe Gallo, Anna Scudellari, Adéle Robberstad, Michelle Chernoff, and Anna-Karin Olofsson.

Lastly, I want to thank whoever threw out that great big oak table on Cathedral Avenue NW in Washington, D.C. It became my perfect writing space, and I hope we'll never part. I expressly do *not* want to thank Windows 8 and wonder how I ever wrote a book with its constant interruptions. And that goes for my little dog, too.

CREDITS

Art Resource: © Museum of the City of New York: 44

© Baddish Group: 6

Corbis: © Bettman: 101

Deposit Photos: © SUMATUSCANI: 182

Courtesy Eric Seed: 174

Everett Collection: 91; © Advertising Archive: 178

Getty Images: © APIC: 89; © Loeffler/P.L. Sperr Collection/Frederic Lewis: 120; © Topical Press Agency/Hulton: xiii

Courtesy Philip Greene: 27, 99

© Historic New Orleans Collection: 23

iStockphoto: © btrenkel: xi

Library of Congress: 33, 40, 46, 60, 74, 97, 149

Redux Pictures: © Hiroko Masuike/**The New York Times:** 204

Shutterstock: © mikecphoto: 194; © Christian Mueller: 214; © Everett Collection: 233

Stocksy: © Tru Studio: 116

© Henri Villard: 17

Courtesy Wikimedia Foundation: 37, 155

RECIPES AND INGREDIENTS INDEX

GENERAL INDEX

Note: *Page numbers in italics indicate/include captions.*